TAPESTRY

PASSAGES

Exploring Spoken English

TAPESTRY

❖

The **Tapestry** program of language materials is based on the concepts presented in *The Tapestry Of Language Learning: The Individual in the Communicative Classroom* by Robin C. Scarcella & Rebecca L. Oxford.

❖

Each title in this program focuses on:

❖

Individual learner strategies and instruction

❖

The relatedness of skills

❖

Ongoing self-assessment

❖

Authentic material as input

❖

Theme-based learning linked to task-based instruction

❖

Attention to all aspects of communicative competence

TAPESTRY

PASSAGES

Exploring Spoken English

Gary James

Heinle & Heinle Publishers
A Division of Wadsworth, Inc.
Boston, Massachusetts, 02116, USA

The publication of *Passages* was directed by the members of the Heinle & Heinle ESL Publishing Team:

David Lee, Editorial Director
Susan Mraz, Marketing Manager
Lisa McLaughlin, Production Editor

Also participating in the publication of this program were:

Publisher: Stanley J. Galek
Editorial Production Manager: Elizabeth Holthaus
Assistant Editor: Kenneth Mattsson
Manufacturing Coordinator: Mary Beth Lynch
Full Service Project Manager/Compositor: Monotype Composition Company
Interior Design: Maureen Lauran
Cover Design: Maureen Lauran

Copyright © 1993 By Heinle & Heinle Publishers

All rights reserved. No part of this publication may be reproduced or transmitted in any form or by any means, electronic or mechanical, including photocopy, recording, or any information storage and retrieval system, without permission in writing from the publisher.

Manufactured in the United States of America.

ISBN: 0-8384-2311-6

Heinle & Heinle Publishers is a division of Wadsworth, Inc.

10 9 8 7 6 5 4 3

To my hanai parents:
Masanori and Shimako Ban
and in memory of
Sharon James

PHOTO CREDITS

4, Karen Preuss/Image Works. 8, Joel Gordon. 21, SuperStock. 35, George Whiteley/Photo Researchers. 45, Spencer Grant/Photo Researchers. 51, Kathleen Campell/AllStock. 55, Barbara Rios/Photo Researchers. 68, John Griffin/Image Works. 76, Joel Gordon. 79, Image Works. 80, Peter Fink/Photo Researchers. 90, Tony Savino/Image Works. 97, Charles Gatewood/Image Works. 104, NASA/Image Works. 118, Joel Gordon. 121, SuperStock/four by five. 125, Joel Gordon.

ILLUSTRATIONS

Susan Jones
Steven Patterson
Steven Blank

Welcome To Tapestry

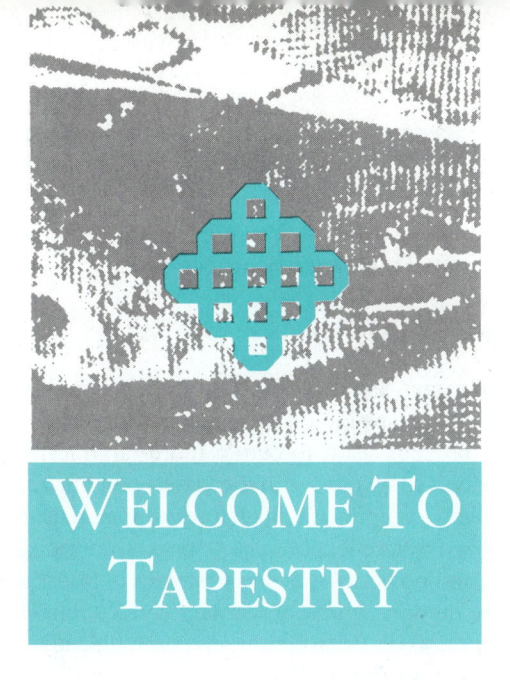

*E*nter the world of Tapestry! Language learning can be seen as an ever-developing tapestry woven with many threads and colors. The elements of the tapestry are related to different language skills like listening and speaking, reading and writing; the characteristics of the teachers; the desires, needs, and backgrounds of the students; and the general second language development process. When all these elements are working together harmoniously, the result is a colorful, continuously growing tapestry of language competence of which the student and the teacher can be proud.

This volume is part of the Tapestry program for students of English as a second language (ESL) at levels from beginning to "bridge" (which follows the advanced level and prepares students to enter regular postsecondary programs along with native English speakers). Tapestry levels include:

Beginning
Low Intermediate
High Intermediate
Low Advanced
High Advanced
Bridge

Because the Tapestry Program provides a unified theoretical and pedagogical foundation for all its components, you can optimally use all the Tapestry student books in a coordinated fashion as an entire curriculum of materials. (They will be published from 1993 to 1995 with further editions likely thereafter.) Alternatively, you can decide to use just certain Tapestry volumes, depending on your specific needs.

Tapestry is primarily designed for ESL students at postsecondary institutions in North America. Some want to learn ESL for academic or career advancement, others for social and personal reasons. Tapestry builds directly on all these motivations. Tapestry stimulates learners to do their best. It enables learners to use English naturally and to develop fluency as well as accuracy.

Tapestry Principles

The following principles underlie the instruction provided in all of the components of the Tapestry program.

EMPOWERING LEARNERS

Language learners in Tapestry classrooms are active and increasingly responsible for developing their English language skills and related cultural abilities. This self-direction leads to better, more rapid learning. Some cultures virtually train their students to be passive in the classroom, but Tapestry weans them from passivity by providing exceptionally high-interest materials, colorful and motivating activities, personalized self-reflection tasks, peer tutoring and other forms of cooperative learning, and powerful learning strategies to boost self-direction in learning.

The empowerment of learners creates refreshing new roles for teachers, too. The teacher serves as facilitator, co-communicator, diagnostician, guide, and helper. Teachers are set free to be more creative at the same time their students become more autonomous learners.

HELPING STUDENTS IMPROVE THEIR LEARNING STRATEGIES

Learning strategies are the behaviors or steps an individual uses to enhance his or her learning. Examples are taking notes, practicing, finding a conversation partner, analyzing words, using background knowledge, and controlling anxiety. Hundreds of such strategies have been identified. Successful language learners use language learning strategies that are most effective for them given their particular learning style, and they put them together smoothly to fit the needs of a given language task. On the other hand, the learning strategies of less successful learners are a desperate grab-bag of ill-matched techniques.

All learners need to know a wide range of learning strategies. All learners need systematic practice in choosing and applying strategies that are relevant for various learning needs. Tapestry is one of the only ESL programs that overtly weaves a comprehensive set of learning strategies into language activities in all its volumes. These learning strategies are arranged in six broad categories throughout the Tapestry books:

- Forming concepts
- Personalizing
- Remembering new material
- Managing your learning
- Understanding and using emotions
- Overcoming limitations

The most useful strategies are sometimes repeated and flagged with a note, "It Works! Learning Strategy . . ." to remind students to use a learning strategy they have already encountered. This recycling reinforces the value of learning strategies and provides greater practice.

RECOGNIZING AND HANDLING LEARNING STYLES EFFECTIVELY

Learners have different learning styles (for instance, visual, auditory, hands-on; reflective, impulsive; analytic, global; extroverted, introverted; closure-oriented, open). Particularly in an ESL setting, where students come from vastly different cultural backgrounds, learning styles differences abound and can cause "style conflicts."

Unlike most language instruction materials, Tapestry provides exciting activities specifically tailored to the needs of students with a large range of learning styles. You can use any Tapestry volume with the confidence that the activities and materials are intentionally geared for many different styles. Insights from the latest educational and psychological research undergird this style-nourishing variety.

OFFERING AUTHENTIC, MEANINGFUL COMMUNICATION

Students need to encounter language that provides authentic, meaningful communication. They must be involved in real-life communication tasks that cause them to *want* and *need* to read, write, speak, and listen to English. Moreover, the tasks—to be most effective—must be arranged around themes relevant to learners.

Themes like family relationships, survival in the educational system, personal health, friendships in a new country, political changes, and protection of the environment are all valuable to ESL learners. Tapestry focuses on topics like these. In every Tapestry volume, you will see specific content drawn from very broad areas such as home life, science and technology, business, humanities, social sciences, global issues, and multiculturalism. All the themes are real and important, and they are fashioned into language tasks that students enjoy.

At the advanced level, Tapestry also includes special books each focused on a single broad theme. For instance, there are two books on business English, two on English for science and technology, and two on academic communication and study skills.

UNDERSTANDING AND VALUING DIFFERENT CULTURES

Many ESL books and programs focus completely on the "new" culture, that is, the culture which the students are entering. The implicit message is that ESL students should just learn about this target culture, and there is no need to understand their own culture better or to find out about the cultures of their international classmates. To some ESL students, this makes them feel their own culture is not valued in the new country.

Tapestry is designed to provide a clear and understandable entry into North American culture. Nevertheless, the Tapestry Program values *all* the cultures found in the ESL classroom. Tapestry students have constant opportunities to become "culturally fluent" in North American culture while they are learning English, but they also have the chance to think about the cultures of their classmates and even understand their home culture from different perspectives.

INTEGRATING THE LANGUAGE SKILLS

Communication in a language is not restricted to one skill or another. ESL students are typically expected to learn (to a greater or lesser degree) all four language skills: reading, writing, speaking, and listening. They are also expected to develop strong grammatical competence, as well as becoming socioculturally sensitive and knowing what to do when they encounter a "language barrier."

Research shows that multi-skill learning is more effective than isolated-skill learning, because related activities in several skills provide reinforcement and refresh the learner's memory. Therefore, Tapestry integrates all the skills. A given Tapestry volume might highlight one skill, such as reading, but all other skills are also included to support and strengthen overall language development.

However, many intensive ESL programs are divided into classes labeled according to one skill (Reading Comprehension Class) or at most two skills (Listening/Speaking Class or Oral Communication Class). The volumes in the Tapestry Program can easily be used to fit this traditional format, because each volume clearly identifies its highlighted or central skill(s).

Grammar is interwoven into all Tapestry volumes. However, there is also a separate reference book for students, *The Tapestry Grammar,* and a Grammar Strand composed of grammar "work-out" books at each of the levels in the Tapestry Program.

Other Features of the Tapestry Program

PILOT SITES

It is not enough to provide volumes full of appealing tasks and beautiful pictures. Users deserve to know that the materials have been pilot-tested. In many ESL series, pilot testing takes place at only a few sites or even just in the classroom of the author. In contrast, Heine & Heinle Publishers have developed a network of Tapestry Pilot Test Sites throughout North America. At this time, there are approximately 40 such sites, although the number grows weekly. These sites try out the materials and provide suggestions for revisions. They are all actively engaged in making Tapestry the best program possible.

AN OVERALL GUIDEBOOK

To offer coherence to the entire Tapestry Program and especially to offer support for teachers who want to understand the principles and practice of Tapestry, we have written a book entitled, *The Tapestry of Language Learning: The Individual in the Communicative Classroom* (Scarcella and Oxford, published in 1992 by Heinle & Heinle).

A Last Word

We are pleased to welcome you to Tapestry! We use the Tapestry principles every day, and we hope these principles—and all the books in the Tapestry Program—provide you the same strength, confidence, and joy that they give us. We look forward to comments from both teachers and students who use any part of the Tapestry Program.

Rebecca L. Oxford
University of Alabama
Tuscaloosa, Alabama

Robin C. Scarcella
University of California at Irvine
Irvine, California

PREFACE

Passages Exploring Spoken English gives intermediate-level students a chance to hear actual language found in the real world outside the ESL classroom. Students are guided through a process of learning how to get ready and how to listen for the most important elements of a passage. Samples of both interactional language (conversations) and transactional language (news broadcasts, lectures, and advertisements) are included. All these passages are authentic bits of language taken from the real world of radio broadcasting, or are from unrehearsed recorded situations resulting in extemporaneously-delivered spoken English.

Complementing the listening passages is related print material taken directly from the real world of newspapers, magazines, newsletters, brochures, and the like. These are used to stimulate reading, writing, and vocabulary and discussion activities both inside and outside the classroom.

Passages: Exploring Spoken English consists of a prologue, eight chapters, and an appendix. Each chapter in *Passages* is divided into three distinct parts.

Before You Listen

These are task-based activities designed to activate students' past knowledge about relevant information, concepts, and vocabulary found in the recordings they hear. Examples of activities found in this part include:

- Guessing (e.g., "What do you think pre-owned means?").
- Surveying (e.g., "Count the number of domestic/imported cars in the school parking lot.")—prior to listening to a mini-lecture on automobiles.
- Brainstorming (e.g., "In 30 seconds list as many words as you can about FAMILY.")—prior to listening to a conversation about families.

As You Listen

These are task-based activities designed to help students use suitable listening strategies as they listen to the passages. Examples of activities found in this part include:

- Getting the Main Idea (e.g., "Which of the three situations represent the one described?")—while listening to a radio call-in talk show.
- Taking Notes (e.g., "List the five sources of our attitudes.")—while listening to a mini-lecture on where our feelings come from.
- Filling In (e.g., "Fill in the grid with the appropriate information about credit cards.")—while listening to a radio ad for credit cards.

After You Listen

These are task-based activities designed to extend students' exposure to the theme of the listening passage through discussion, reading, writing (Following Up/Just for Fun), and vocabulary practice (Word Study).

An integral part of *Passages* involves the overt teaching of learning strategies. The various tasks which students are directed to perform throughout the text are labeled with an appropriate strategy. At the end of each chapter, students and instructor alike assess progress in the use of these learning strategies.

Another important feature is found in the Appendix section under the title Each One/Teach One. Following Chapter 4, student groups are provided new listening passages similar to the ones they have been working with in Chapters 1–4 (a conversation, an advertisement, news stories, and mini-lectures). Groups choose an individual passage and work together as separate teams to put together a unit of study based on that passage for end-of-the-term presentation to the rest of the class. The instructor's resource manual gives a more detailed explanation.

Still another essential part of *Passages* is an assessment component. Six quizzes are provided for use following Chapter 1, Chapter 3, Chapter 4, Chapter 6, Chapter 7, and Chapter 8. Information and suggestions for their use are also found in the manual along with ideas about how to create and maintain individual student portfolios (composed of quiz results, periodic student/instructor assessments, and student-generated audiotapes).

Acknowledgements

Passages: Exploring Spoken English represents a radical departure from the kinds of textbooks I have written in the past. There are many who need to be acknowledged for assisting me in my "passage" from the old to the new.

I am profoundly grateful to Dave Lee, Editorial Director at Heinle & Heinle, for inspiring me to try out different ways of doing things. He has become a treasured friend in the process. Heinle's assistant editor, Ken Mattsson, was always understanding and helpful, but most importantly, always there when needed. Rebecca Oxford, Robin Scarcella, and Bob Oprandy provided invaluable on-target critiques and helpful suggestions from the beginning. Conversations and exchanges of information with Mary Gill, Pam Hartmann, and Maggie Sokolik made the creative process an easier one. Christy Ban, a real one-person clipping service, supplied me with a wealth of theme-related information from magazines and newspapers. I am indebted to the following print media for permitting me to use information from their pages: *Action Magazine, Associated Press, Changing Times, Gannett News Service, Honolulu Advertiser, Honolulu Star-Bulletin, Honolulu Weekly, Knight-Ridder Tribune News Service, McCall's, New York Times, Reuters News Service, San Francisco Chronicle,* and *Tribune Media Services.* Chuck Whitley allowed me to use his exercise on adjectives in Chapter 5. In that regard, my long association with both Chuck and Sharon Bode has unquestionably been a learning experience few other materials writers have enjoyed. I owe them much more than they will ever know. The coming together of an ELI "team" at Honolulu Community College made up of Muriel Fujii, Lei Lani Hinds, and Chuck Whitley allowed me the luxury of finding time to create these materials. I am appreciative to Bob Gibson for the origination of "strip story" techniques which have been used here and there in the text. I have often thought he has not been given the credit he is due for the idea.

I would also like to thank Debra Dean (University of Akron) and Steven Horowitz (Central Washington University) for their helpful comments during the development of this book. Additionally, I thank Jeff Brom (California State University, Los Angeles) and Gary Wood (Portland State University) and their ESL students for testing the material in their classrooms.

Elton Ogoso provided technical facilities and expertise for many of the recordings. Honolulu radio stations, KHPR and KHVH, both kindly allowed for use of material from their airwaves. Colleagues who lent their talents to audiotaping lectures and conversations include: Sharon Bode, George Dixon, Terry Haney, Jim King, Lynnette King, Doric Little, Bette Matthews, Maureen O'Brien, and Chuck Whitley. Kathy Langaman really outdid herself this time with word processing skills and efforts far beyond the call of duty. Finally, no text would exist without the love and support of Paul Ban.

Gary James
Honolulu Community College
Honolulu, Hawaii

Contents

Prologue 1

PASSAGE: HOW NOT TO LISTEN
Before You Listen 2
As You Listen 3
After You Listen 4
   Word Study 5
   Just for Fun 8

1 Living in the U.S. 9

WHAT'S YOUR GOAL

PASSAGE A: CAMPING PERMITS
Before You Listen 11
As You Listen 13
After You Listen 14

PASSAGE B: FAMILY
Before You Listen 15
As You Listen 16
After You Listen 17
   Word Study 17
   Following Up 20
   Just for Fun 21

2 Working 23

WHAT'S YOUR GOAL

PASSAGE A: RANKING OF OCCUPATIONS
Before You Listen 24
As You Listen 27
After You Listen 28

PASSAGE B: WORKING AT HOME
Before You Listen 32
As You Listen 33
After You Listen 33
   Word Study 34
   Following Up 35
   Just for Fun 36

3 Buying and Selling 39

WHAT'S YOUR GOAL

THEME 1: PASSAGE A: CREDIT CARDS
Before You Listen 40
As You Listen 42

xv

THEME 1: PASSAGE B: CREDIT CARDS

Before You Listen	42
As You Listen	43
After You Listen	44
Word Study	44
Following Up	45

THEME 2: PASSAGE A: IMPORTED CARS

Before You Listen	48
As You Listen	49
After You Listen	51
Word Study	55

THEME 2: PASSAGE B: POPULATION CATEGORIES

Before You Listen	56
As You Listen	58
After You Listen	58

4 Keeping Healthy   63

WHAT'S YOUR GOAL

PASSAGE A: MAMMOGRAPHY

Before You Listen	64
As You Listen	65
After You Listen	67

PASSAGE B: IMMUNIZATION

Before You Listen	68
As You Listen	69
After You Listen	69
Word Study	71
Following Up	73
Just for Fun	73

5 Thinking about Feelings   75

WHAT'S YOUR GOAL

PASSAGE A: SOURCES OF ATTITUDES

Before You Listen	76
As You Listen	79
After You Listen	79
Word Study	80

PASSAGE B: AGING

Before You Listen	82
As You Listen	82
After You Listen	83
Word Study	83
Just for Fun	85

6 Thinking about the Society   87

WHAT'S YOUR GOAL

PASSAGE A: HOMELESS PEOPLE

Before You Listen	88
As You Listen	90
After You Listen	90

PASSAGE B: GUN CONTROL

Before You Listen	94
As You Listen	95
After You Listen	96
Word Study	96
Following Up	97

7 Saving the Planet   101

WHAT'S YOUR GOAL

PASSAGE A: HOT WATER HEATING
Before You Listen	102
As You Listen	105
After You Listen	106

PASSAGE B: FUEL CONSUMPTION
Before You Listen	108
As You Listen	109
After You Listen	109
Word Study	109
Following Up	111
Just for Fun	113

8 Learning to Learn   115

WHAT'S YOUR GOAL

PASSAGE A: PLACES TO STUDY
Before You Listen	116
As You Listen	117
After You Listen	118
Word Study	118

PASSAGE B: PLACES TO STUDY
Before You Listen	121
As You Listen	121
After You Listen	122
Word Study	122

PASSAGE C: STUDY SYSTEMS
Before You Listen	124
As You Listen	124
After You Listen	126
Following Up	126

Appendix: EachOne/Teach One   129

Before You Listen	131
As You Listen	132
After You Listen	133
Following Up	134
Just for Fun	135

Prologue

PASSAGE

Before You Listen

LEARNING STRATEGY

Understanding and Using Emations: Discussing your feelings helps you to understand yourself and others.

TASK 1

These students are listening to a lecture in a classroom. What do you think they are doing and thinking? Why?

1. _____
2. _____
3. _____

LEARNING STRATEGY

Forming Concepts: Guessing promotes your language comprehension.

2

TASK 2

You will hear a mini-lecture about listening. Look at the following list of words. Practice saying them. Which words do you think that you will hear? Why? Discuss your answers.

active	lecture	subject
criticizing	lecturer	summarize
dull	main ideas	talks
faking attention	mental movies	topic
form	message	visualize
goal	overhear	wasting thought
goes down	overreacting	speed
group . . . together	pay attention	words
information	speaker	yielding to distractions
jot down		

> **Threads**
>
> There are 3565 college and universities in the United States.
>
> *U.S. Department of Education*

As You Listen

LEARNING STRATEGY

Managing Your Learning: Checking off vocabulary items as they are heard increases your attention and comprehension.

TASK 3

Look at the vocabulary list in Task 2. Listen to the mini-lecture. Underline the words or phrases that you hear. Discuss your choices.

LEARNING STRATEGY

Forming Concepts: Figuring out the main idea helps you understand better.

TASK 4

This mini-lecture has two main ideas. Read the sentences on page 4. Put an X in front of the two most important points. Discuss your choices.

_____ 1. There are many ways to harm your listening ability.

_____ 2. Calling a subject dull is not a good way to listen.

_____ 3. Listening only to easy things is not a good way to listen.

_____ 4. People can think much faster than they can listen.

_____ 5. Having a clear idea of what your goal is will help you become a better listener.

LEARNING STRATEGY

Remembering New Material: Learning how to take good notes helps you remember what is said in lectures.

TASK 5

Listen again to the mini-lecture and take notes on the ten ways you can harm your listening ability. Compare your notes with a classmate's notes.

1. _____
2. _____
3. _____
4. _____
5. _____
6. _____
7. _____
8. _____
9. _____
10. _____

After You Listen

Following Up

TASK 6

Look back at your notes. Cross out the words that are not necessary. Use abbreviations and symbols when possible. Talk with a classmate about how you take notes.

TASK 7

Look at the ten ways to harm your listening mentioned by the lecturer. Which ones do you *often* do? Mark with an **0**. Which do you *sometimes* do? Mark with a ✓. Which do you *rarely* or *never* do? Mark with an **X**. Compare and discuss your answers with a partner.

Word Study

TASK 8

The words on the left are from the mini-lecture. Practice saying them. Match the words with their definitions on the right, and write the correct letter in the space. Discuss your answers.

____ 1. briefly   a. and so on

____ 2. unusual   b. a short time

____ 3. designed   c. boring

____ 4. stuff   d. causing strong feelings

____ 5. emotional   e. college/university offering bachelor's degrees

____ 6. further   f. finding fault with

____ 7. four-year institution   g. giving in

____ 8. in effect   h. made

____ 9. poor   i. more

____ 10. expert   j. not common

____ 11. what have you   k. not good

____ 12. in other words   l. pretending

____ 13. dull   m. really

____ 14. criticizing   n. someone having special knowledge

____ 15. faking   o. things

____ 16. yielding   p. using wrongly

____ 17. wasting   q. which is the same as saying

> **Threads**
>
> The world's youngest college graduate was William Thompson, who graduated from Glasgow University (Scotland) when he was 10 years, 5 months.
>
> *Guinness Book of World Records (1992)*

PROLOGUE

TASK 9

Practice saying these words from the lecture. Some are nouns, some are verbs. Notice that the spellings are the same.

NOUNS	VERBS
1. design	design
2. hate	hate
3. cough	cough
4. focus	focus
5. transfer	transfer
6. fake	fake
7. waste	waste
8. talk	talk
9. harm	harm
10. blame	blame
11. pace	pace

LEARNING STRATEGY

Remembering New Material: Fitting words into meaningful sentences helps you remember them.

TASK 10

Read the following sentences. Write the correct forms of the words in the blanks. *Be careful—word endings might change.* Word number one on the list (design) goes in sentence number one, word number two goes in sentence number two, and so forth. If the word is a noun, circle the word "noun" located below the blank; if the word is a verb, circle the word "verb."

1. a. Good notes are _____ to help us take tests better.
       noun   verb
   b. The _____ of the test was a good one.
       noun   verb
2. a. _____ is the subject of today's psychology lecture.
       noun   verb
   b. I _____ what the teacher is wearing.
       noun   verb
3. a. A _____ is a kind of distraction in the classroom.
       noun   verb
   b. She _____ in the middle of the lecture.
       noun   verb

4. a. The _____ of the class will be how to listen.
             noun   verb

   b. Try to _____ on what the speaker is saying.
          noun   verb

5. a. He will _____ to a four-year institution next fall.
           noun   verb

   b. How many _____ from other colleges are there?
            noun   verb

6. a. Don't _____ attention while listening to lectures.
           noun   verb

   b. He does not know what he is talking about. He is a _____ .
                                                                                   noun   verb

7. a. It is a _____ not to think about what a speaker is saying.
           noun   verb

   b. Many students _____ their thought speed.
                     noun   verb

8. a. I would like to _____ to you about listening.
                  noun   verb

   b. My _____ will be about better listening habits.
         noun   verb

9. a. There are many ways to _____ your listening ability.
                               noun   verb

   b. What _____ come from plagiarism?
           noun   verb

10. a. Please don't _____ me for your bad grade.
                   noun   verb

    b. The _____ for the bad grade is yours.
           noun   verb

11. a. Her _____ across the campus was faster than I thought.
           noun   verb

    b. It bothers me to watch the teacher _____ back and forth.
                                            noun   verb

> **Threads**
>
> "I have never let my schooling interfere with my education."
>
> Mark Twain (1835–1910)

LEARNING STRATEGY

Remembering New Material: Associating new words to other words helps you to remember vocabulary.

Read and discuss the following questions with your classmates.

TASK 11

"*Overreacting*" means "acting in a way stronger than necessary." How many other words can you think of that begin with "*over-*" and mean "to do something too much." For example, "overdo," "overgrow," and "overstay."

TASK 12

The lecturer said that listening is a *tool* to help us take tests. What other tools can you think of for the following list of activities:

- getting to class on time
- finding the meaning of a word
- making a daily time schedule
- writing a five-hundred-word essay

TASK 13

The lecturer said that while listening you should not overreact to *emotional* words. Can you think of some examples of emotional words?

Just for Fun

LEARNING STRATEGY

Understanding and Using Emotions: Laughing and having a good time while learning can increase your chances of learning a language well.

TASK 14

Everybody fakes attention sometimes. Be honest and tell what you do when you want to fake attention.

TASK 15

People from different cultures use different gestures/body movements and words/sounds to show a speaker they are listening. How do people in *your* country let each other know they are listening? Make a list and compare it with each other's list.

GESTURES/BODY MOVEMENTS	WORDS/SOUNDS
1. _____	1. _____
2. _____	2. _____
3. _____	3. _____

TASK 16

Spend time outside the classroom watching people talk to each other in a park, on a street corner, in a sitcom on TV, in a movie, etc. Make a list of gestures/body movements and words/sounds that you observe. Share these observations with your classmates.

Living in the U.S.

CHAPTER 1

LEARNING STRATEGY

Managing Your Learning: Thinking about what you want to accomplish before doing it helps you do it better.

WHAT'S YOUR GOAL?

Look at the following six goals for Chapter 1. Which is the most important one for you? Mark it (1). How about the second most important? Mark it (2), etc.

I WANT TO LEARN HOW TO	RANK
A. remember what I hear	_____
B. understand what I hear	_____
C. express myself even though I don't know all the words	_____
D. organize and assess what I hear and say	_____
E. speak and listen to others about personal feelings or views	_____
F. learn with other people	_____

PASSAGE A

Before You Listen

LEARNING STRATEGY

Managing Your Learning: Working with other language learners helps you improve language skills.

TASK 1

Look at the following months. Each one has holidays when many American families get together and do things. Work with a partner and list the holidays.

January _____

May _____

July _____

September _____

October _____

November _____

December _____

TASK 2

Look at the following activities. Which ones go with the holidays in Task 1? Talk about your answers.

barbecuing	eating	sailing
camping	fishing	skating
collecting candy and fruit	picnicking	skiing
cycling	playing games	swimming

TASK 3

Ask a partner about his/her family's favorite holiday. Find out what the family does on that day. Take notes so you can later report your findings to the class.

11

LEARNING STRATEGY

Overcoming Limitations: Participating in relevant activities in the classroom helps you in the real world.

TASK 4

Pretend that you and your family want to go camping. Sometimes you need to fill out an application form for a permit to do this. Why? What other activities do you know that require a permit? Fill in the application below and compare yours with your classmates' applications.

(Use for Camping, Pavilion, Special Use & Picnic Permits)

APPLICATION FOR STATE PARK PERMITS (Please Print)

To be filled in by State Parks
Permit No. _____ Campsite No. _____

TYPE OF PERMIT: Check one:
____ Camping   ____ Pavilion   ____ Special Use: Type _____   ____ Picnic

ISLAND: _____   **Park:** _____

NO. OF PEOPLE: For Camping: Age 18 or Older _____   Under Age 18 _____
   For Other Types of Permits: Total _____

REQUESTED DATES: From _____   To _____

REQUESTED TIMES: (Not required for camping permits)   From _____   To _____

PERMITTEE: #1 Individual   Last Name _____   First Name _____
                                  ID Number _____
         O R
         #2 Organization _____   Contact Person _____

LIST NAMES AND IDs OF OTHER CAMPERS TO BE COVERED BY THIS PERMIT (18 years or older):
(Acceptable identification are Driver's License, Social Sec. Card, State ID, Passport)

NAME	ID NUMBER	NAME	ID NUMBER
_____	_____	_____	_____
_____	_____	_____	_____
_____	_____	_____	_____
_____	_____	_____	_____
_____	_____	_____	_____
_____	_____	_____	_____
_____	_____	_____	_____

ADDRESS _____
              Street   City   State   Zip Code

PHONE: Business: Area Code (___) _____   Home: Area Code (___) _____

 # OF PARKING PERMITS: (_____)   Required for parks camping permits. Max. 5 parking permits for 10 peo. capacity campsite, 2 permits for 5 cap. site.)

EMERGENCY CONTACT: _____   Phone: Area Code (___) _____

PASSAGE A

TASK 5

Now read the following sentences about a news story that you are going to hear. What does each sentence mean?

1. Camping permits are issued twice a year.
2. People camp out to get camping permits.
3. Waiting children are playing cards.
4. The people who are waiting are not homeless.

As You Listen

LEARNING STRATEGY

Forming Concepts: Get the main idea.

TASK 6

Listen to the news story. Which sentence above is the main idea (most important point) of the story?

TASK 7

What do the following sentences mean? Listen to the news story again. Mark the following statements either TRUE or FALSE. Change each false statement to make it true. Work together with a partner.

_____ 1. The State Parks Division issues permits for camping.

_____ 2. People waited in line for a few minutes.

_____ 3. The people waiting in line were happy.

_____ 4. The people waiting in line were standing up.

_____ 5. The people were eating, drinking, and talking.

_____ 6. There are permits for 219 camping sites.

_____ 7. The permits are for Memorial Day and Independence Day weekends.

_____ 8. Sue Sheldon waited in line for three days.

> **Threads**
>
> The average size of a household in the U.S. has changed from 3.3 in 1960 to 2.63 in 1990.
>
> U.S. Bureau of the Census

After You Listen

Read the following general park rules campers must follow. Talk about any items you do not know with your classmates.

General Park Rules

Help us protect your state parks. Park rules are designed to help you and others have an enjoyable and fulfilling visit and to protect the cultural and natural resources for future generations. You can help us accomplish both aims by observing the following rules.

ALCOHOLIC BEVERAGES. The use or possession of alcoholic beverages is prohibited.

BEGGING AND SOLICITING are prohibited.

BOATING VESSELS or any similar buoyant devices are prohibited where posted.

FIRES: Build fires in the fireplaces and grills provided. Portable stoves or warming devices may be used in designated camping and picnicking areas unless otherwise prohibited.

LOST AND FOUND ARTICLES are to be deposited by the finder at the nearest police station.

METAL DETECTING DEVICES are allowed on sand beaches only. Their use or possession elsewhere is prohibited.

NATURAL AND CULTURAL FEATURES: Leave all geologic, historic and archaeological features undisturbed.

NUDITY is prohibited.

PETS and other animals are to be crated, caged, on a 6-foot or shorter leash or otherwise under physical restrictive control at all times and are not permitted in restaurants, pavilions, swimming areas, campgrounds, lodges, on beaches and wherever posted. Horses prohibited unless otherwise posted. Please clean up after your pet.

PLANTS: Leave all plant life undisturbed. Where permitted, reasonable quantities of fruits and seeds may be gathered for personal use.

REPORT OF INJURY OR DAMAGE: All incidents resulting in personal injury or death, or property damage must be reported as soon as possible to the district office, and other appropriate agencies.

SKATING AND SKATEBOARDS are prohibited where posted.

VEHICLES: Drive and park motor vehicles only on designated roads and parking areas provided for such use.

WASTE DISPOSAL: Place all waste materials in trash cans.

WILDLIFE: Leave the wildlife and their habitat undisturbed except where hunting and fishing is permitted subject to all applicable laws and regulations.

SUSPECTED VIOLATIONS: Report suspected law and park rule violations to enforcement officers, call the Conservation Hotline "548-5918." Or contact the Division of Conservation and Resources Enforcement's district office; after hours, on weekends and on holidays, dial "0" and ask for "Enterprise 5469."

For more information on the regulation and control of the State Park System consult Rules of the Hawaii State Park System at the district office.

PASSAGE B

Before You Listen

LEARNING STRATEGY

Managing Your Learning: Making lists of relevant vocabulary helps you get ready for upcoming language tasks.

TASK 8

What does FAMILY mean to you? Brainstorm for two minutes. List all the words you can think of that are associated with FAMILY. Compare your list with those of your classmates.

_____
_____
_____
_____
_____
_____
_____
_____

> **Threads**
>
> According to the U.S. Census figures, one-third of all marriages that produce children in the U.S. end in divorce.

TASK 9

Now using the words from the list above, write five *either/or* questions to ask your partner about his/her family. Ask about number of people, closest/oldest/youngest family members, etc.

1. _Are you closer to your mother or to your father?_____
2. _____
3. _____
4. _____
5. _____

LIVING IN THE U.S.

TASK 10

Ask your partner the above questions and write answers on the lines below.

1. _____
2. _____
3. _____
4. _____
5. _____

TASK 11

Compare *your* family with your *partner's* family. Report your findings to the class.

TASK 12

Look at the following four topics. Talk about what each one means.

1. Family reunions
2. How to have close family relationships
3. Family activities
4. Family relationships

Threads

On October 3, 1992, the Rails to Trails Conservancy celebrated the opening of its 500th bike and pedestrian trail in Massachusetts.

*IT WORKS!
Learning Strategy:
Managing Your
Learning*

As You Listen

TASK 13

Now listen to Lynnette and Gary's conversation. What was the main subject of the discussion? Choose one from the list above. Talk about your answers.

TASK 14

Listen to the discussion again and decide how both speakers feel about the following topics. Circle the answer.

TOPIC	FEELINGS	
Aunts/Uncles/Cousins	CLOSE	NOT CLOSE
Family Reunions	LIKE	DO NOT LIKE
Mother's Relatives	CLOSE	NOT CLOSE
Father's Relatives	CLOSE	NOT CLOSE

PASSAGE B

After You Listen

Word Study

TASK 15

Look at these verbs taken from the listening passages. Talk about their meanings. Practice saying them.

| issue | file | celebrate | resent |
| assure | secure | hate | |

IT WORKS!
Learning Strategy:
Remembering New
Material

TASK 16

Now combine the verbs listed above with the following phrases as in number 1. There are at least two phrases for each verb and sometimes more. Talk about what each one means.

an agreement	camping permits
a good camping spot	funerals
a news story	holidays
a seat in the front row	marriage licenses
a traffic ticket	relatives
birthdays	reunions
brothers and sisters	this report

1. _issue marriage licenses_
2. _____
3. _____
4. _____
5. _____
6. _____
7. _____
8. _____
9. _____
10. _____
11. _____
12. _____
13. _____
14. _____

LEARNING STRATEGY

Remembering New Material: Arranging new words with other related words is a good way to remember vocabulary.

TASK 17

A word map is a diagram showing how words are related and connected to each other. Look at the word map for things that you can *participate in*. You can *participate in school* by taking an *English class* which is divided into *groups*. You can also *participate in school* by joining *clubs* and being on *committees* in the club. Work with a partner and try to complete the word map by adding as many words as you can.

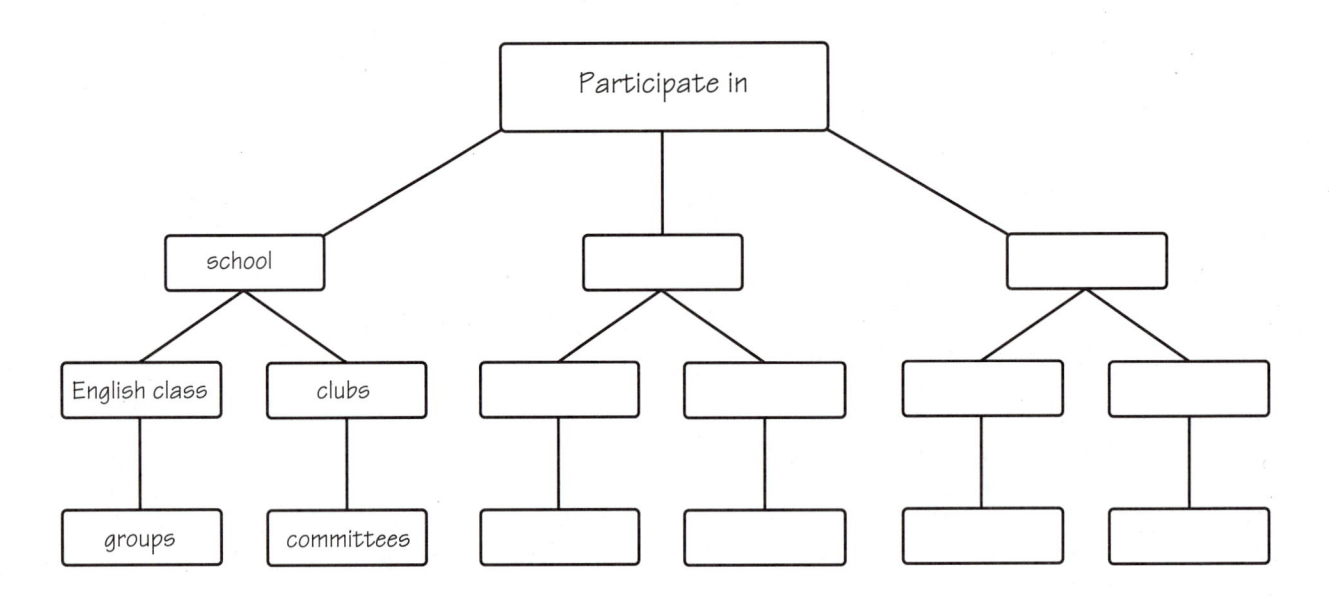

```
                    Participate in
         ┌──────────────┼──────────────┐
       school          ___            ___
       ┌──┴──┐       ┌──┴──┐        ┌──┴──┐
  English   clubs   ___   ___      ___   ___
  class      │       │     │        │     │
     │    committees ___   ___      ___   ___
   groups
```

TASK 18

Practice saying these words from the listening passages. Some are nouns and some are verbs. Notice that the forms are exactly the same.

NOUNS	VERBS
1. lounge	lounge
2. permit	permit
3. issue	issue
4. highlight	highlight
5. camp	camp
6. spot	spot
7. file	file
8. share	share

TASK 19

PASSAGE B

IT WORKS!
Learning Strategy:
Remembering New
Material

Read the following sentences. Write the correct form of the word from task 18 in the blank. Word number one on the list (lounge) goes in sentence number one, word number two goes in sentence number two, etc. If the word is a noun, circle the word "noun" located below the blank; if the word is a verb, circle the word "verb." *Be careful—word forms might change*.

1. a. All kinds of activities take place in the student _____ .
      noun   verb

   b. Don't _____ around near the office door.
      noun   verb

2. a. My parents would not _____ me to go.
      noun   verb

   b. You need a _____ to carry a gun.
      noun   verb

3. a. How long does it take for the state to _____ a driver's license?
      noun   verb

   b. Which _____ of the newspaper is the story in?
      noun   verb

4. a. One of the _____ of my childhood was going to summer camp.
      noun   verb

   b. Please _____ the main idea with a yellow marking pen.
      noun

5. a. Let's go and _____ on the beach this weekend.
      noun   verb

   b. The only thing I didn't like about the _____ were the mosquitoes.
      noun   verb

6. a. Did you _____ any smoke on the horizon?
      noun   verb

   b. She found a good _____ for the camp.
      noun   verb

7. a. I put your application in the _____ cabinet.
      noun   verb

   b. Why don't you _____ that information away until next year?
      noun   verb

8. a. I will pay for my _____ of the bill.
      noun   verb

   b. My parents taught the children in the family how to _____ things.
      noun   verb

Threads

"We are the people who have the hardest time slowing down enough to fully appreciate the relaxed art of dining."

–John Robbins from *May All Be Fed: Diet for a New World*, William Morrow & Co. (1992)

LIVING IN THE U.S.

Following Up

TASK 20

Read the discussion suggestions and choose one to talk or write about. After you finish, present your views to the rest of the class.

- Neither of the speakers has a close relationship with family members outside their immediate family. Do you feel the same way about your family? Why? If you are close to a particular family member outside your immediate family, tell why this is so and compare your experiences with your classmates.
- One of the speakers asked the other if he thought there were advantages to getting together in large family groups and having closer relationships. How would you answer this question? Give reasons for your answer and discuss them.
- Over the years American families have changed a lot. Previously, a family usually meant a married woman and man with children. Nowadays it is common to see families consisting of single parents and children. A family can also mean an unmarried woman and man who live together. For some, a family means same-sex partners in a lesbian or gay relationship. How would you define the meaning of family? Have you changed your ideas recently? Why?

LEARNING STRATEGY

Understanding and Using Emotions: Comparing your feelings with others promotes understanding.

TASK 21

Read the following news story about husbands and wives in Japan. Is the situation the same in your country? If you are from Japan, is the situation the same in your family? In a group of four of five, talk about your feelings with your classmates.

Survey: Japanese husbands of little help to wives at home

TOKYO—Most Japanese men in their 40s are too lazy to do such simple tasks as clearing the table and making their beds, leaving the chores to their wives, a survey released today said.

More than 70 percent of middle-age husbands polled were too lazy to make their beds, clear the table after meals or put away newspapers, the survey by the Leisure Development Center showed.

The center questioned 200 middle-age couples on their life styles and values.

About 60 percent of husbands polled were reluctant to take part in domestic chores such as shopping and preparing meals.

Women said they would like their husbands to help more but described routine domestic chores such as cooking as a wife's job, said a spokeswoman at the center, an affiliate of the Ministry of International Trade and Industry.

Reuters News Service

TASK 22

PASSAGE B

It is common in Latino cultures (and many others) for whole generations of families to live together in one house or apartment. For example, a typical household might consist of parents and children plus grandparents, aunts, uncles, etc. Talk about who you live with. Compare living situations.

Just for Fun

TASK 23

- Form groups of ten or fewer. If there are fifteen members in the class, break up into groups of eight and seven, and so forth.
- Your instructor will give each of you a strip of paper with a sentence or phrase on it. The words make up a story about a father who lives with his married daughter. Read the words and memorize them. Don't show your words to anyone. Don't write down the words.
- The instructor will collect the strips. Now work together and try to combine the sentences and phrases into the complete story. Use only your listening and speaking abilities.

LEARNING STRATEGY

Managing Your Learning: Evaluating past learning efforts enables you to be more successful in future language learning.

Name _____

Date _____

Now look at the following checklist of language learning strategies from Chapter 1. How would you assess your progress in the use of each one? Use the following symbols:

S = satisfied with progress

D = still developing

Compare yours with the instructor's assessments.

LEARNING STRATEGY	MY ASSESSMENT	INSTRUCTOR'S ASSESSMENT
I am learning how to:		
remember what I hear (remembering new material)	_____	_____
understand what I hear (forming concepts)	_____	_____
express myself even though I don't know all the words (overcoming limitations)	_____	_____
organize and assess what I hear and say (managing your learning)	_____	_____
speak and listen to others about personal feelings or views (understanding and using emotions)	_____	_____
learn with other people (managing your learning understanding and using emotions)	_____	_____

Working

CHAPTER 2

WHAT'S YOUR GOAL?

IT WORKS!
Learning Strategy:
Managing Your
Learning

Look at the following six goals for Chapter 2. Which is the most important one for you? Mark it (1). How about the second most important? Mark it (2), etc.

I WANT TO LEARN HOW TO:	RANK
A. remember what I hear	_____
B. understand what I hear	_____
C. express myself even though I don't know all the words	_____
D. organize and assess what I hear and say	_____
E. speak and listen to others about personal feelings or views	_____
F. learn with other people	_____

PASSAGE A

Before You Listen

TASK 1

With a partner look at the pictures on pages 25-27. Identify the occupation of each person. Tell what each person does. The first one is done for you.

25

PASSAGE A

A.

An athlete
plays sports.

B.

C.

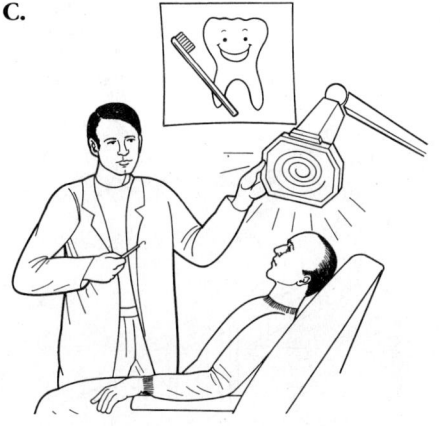

D.

E.

F.

26

CHAPTER 2 WORKING

G.

H.

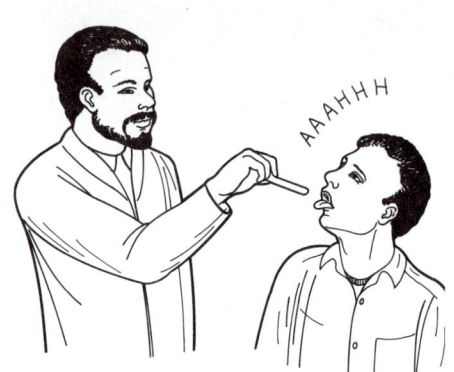

I.

J.

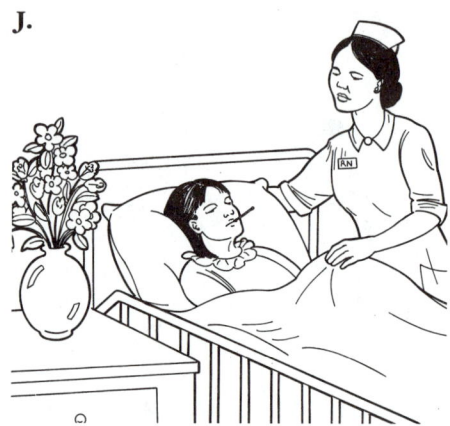

Threads

Ninty percent of Americans pay higher taxes now than in 1990.

Citizens for Tax Justice

K.

L.

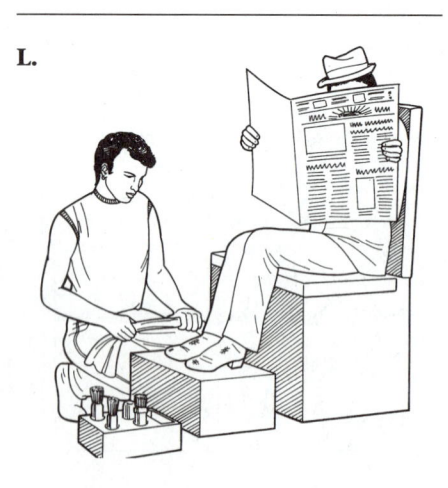

M.

_____

_____

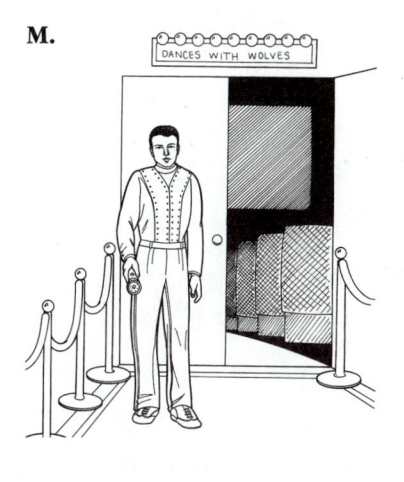

TASK 2

Look at the occupations illustrated in Task 1. Mark the ones you admire the most with a plus sign (+), the least with a minus sign (-), and those in between with a check mark (✓). Why do you feel the way you do? Discuss your feelings with your classmates.

IT WORKS!
Learning Strategy:
Understanding and
Using Emotions

LEARNING STRATEGY

Forming Concepts: Figuring out answers to questions using your past knowledge is an important part of learning.

TASK 3

Of all the occupations, which *four* require the most formal education, taking courses in math, science, etc.? Mark the four above with an asterisk (*).

As You Listen

TASK 4

Listen to the mini-lecture. It tells how the general public feels about certain jobs. See if the results of the survey given in the lecture match your own feelings. Take notes in the space provided on page 28 while you listen. Use abbreviations. Compare your notes with a partner.

CHAPTER 2 WORKING

OCCUPATIONS	RANKING
_____	_____
_____	_____
_____	_____
_____	_____
_____	_____
_____	_____
_____	_____
_____	_____

> **Threads**
>
> In 1830, 70.5% of workers in America worked on farms. By 1980, it was 2.2%.
>
> U.S. Bureau of the Census

TASK 5

Put an ascending mark (↑) next to those occupations you would rank higher and a descending mark (↓) next to those you and you partner would rank lower. Report your opinions to the rest of the class.

After You Listen

TASK 6

Are there other occupations not given in the mini-lecture that are considered very high in your country? Very low? In between? Why? Compare your ideas with your classmates'.

TASK 7

Look at the graphic on page 29 that lists the fastest growing jobs in the U.S. In groups of three or four, talk about the following:

- What kind of background and preparation do many of the jobs call for?
- Would you be interested in any of these jobs? Why or why not?

LEARNING STRATEGY

Forming Concepts: Using what you already know helps you understand new information.

Fastest Growing Jobs Growth Rate, 1990–2005

Job	%
• Home health aide	92%
• Paralegal	85
Systems analyst	79
Personal aide	77
Physical therapist	76
• Medical assistant	74
Operations research analyst	73
• Human services worker	71
• Radiologic technician/technologist	70
• Medical secretary	68
• Physical therapy aide	64
Psychologist	64
• Travel agent	62
Correction worker	61
• Data processing equipment repairer	60
Flight attendant	59
Computer programmer	56
Occupational therapist	55
Management analyst	52
• Medical equipment repairer	51
• Child care worker	49
• Information clerk	47
• Legal secretary	47
Marketing, advertising, p.r. manager	47
Podiatrist	46
Registered nurse	44
• Therapist	44
• Nursing aide	43
• Restaurant cook	42
• Health technician	42
• Licensed practical nurse	42
• Preschool teacher	41
Private detective	41
Producer/actor	41

Threads

The fastest growing field for the 1990s is expected to be medical assistants, with a 70% increase from 1988.

U.S. Bureau of Labor Statistics

CHAPTER 2 WORKING

TASK 8

Look at the following list of jobs. With a partner, circle the ones which require the most technical and scientific backgrounds.

OCCUPATION	STARTING SALARY
Accounting clerk	
Air traffic controller	
Architect	
Bank teller	
Biologist	
Carpenter	
Chemist	
Computer Scientist	
Dentist	
Elementary school teacher	
Engineer	
Environmental engineer	
Geologist	
Lawyer (private industry)	
Mechanical engineer	
Nursing	
Petroleum engineer	
Pharmacist	
Pilot (captain)	
Secretary	
Typist	
Veterinarian	
Word processor	

TASK 9

Work together and estimate the starting salaries for the occupations above. Write your guesses on the lines. Compare your findings with your classmates' findings. Then check actual salaries in the answer key.

> **Threads**
>
> Bette Nesmith Graham began to cover her typing mistakes with white paint because she was a poor typist. This product later became Liquid Paper®.

TASK 10

Read the following newspaper feature article on an occupation which is uncommon. How would you like this person's job?

Charles Clark has been an embalmer for seven years and he's heard 'em all. Still, he can't tell you often enough how important it is to keep a sense of humor in his business.

As an embalmer, Clark prepares all kinds of bodies for burial: old and young, healthy and ravaged, victims of accidents, suicides, diseases and time. He spends his days suited up in goggles, gloves, shoe covers, a barrier mask, a head cover, a face shield, an apron and a coverall, staving off the withering of the flesh with an exotic combination of chemicals, fluids and tools.

Embalming, Clark says, consists of many things—preserving the body, fixing accident cases, doing make-up, doing hair—"just basically making the individual look really nice, like how you look today. Basically we preserve the remains for public viewing and make sure the family is happy."

Clark has a pragmatic approach to his work. Slasher movies can't show him anything he hasn't already seen, he says—like the suicide in Waikiki where an unfortunately placed ledge caused the head to wind up on the fourth floor, the body on the first. Or the friend who was run over by a garbage truck and was so "smashed, just crunched like a cardboard box" that Clark was unable to recognize him. "I saw his family and I said 'Oh, how are you? What are you doing here?' His mother said, 'My son's in the back.' I said to myself, 'I know this guy.' So I went behind and when I opened the sheet up, from the coroner's office, I said 'Oh, my God!' she said, 'Can you really try and put him back together?' I said, 'Well, we'll see what we can do.' But it was really . . . He was just smashed." Clark hits the table. "Like a pancake, you know?"

Clark was born and raised in Kalihi, "by Kenny's Burger House." When he was a junior in high school he got a job cutting grass for Borthwick Mortuary and one thing led to another. He worked doing "removals" (picking up remains), cleaning the chapel, covering the night shift, helping in the prep room. Eventually he trained to become an embalmer. "I was brought up to be scared of funeral homes," he remembers. "But after awhile it didn't bother me. My family told me, 'You're gonna get bad dreams, the spirits are going to come for you.' I said, 'Why are they gonna come for me? I'm the guy that's helping them.'"

Today Clark considers himself part social worker, part scientist. He says he enjoys the challenge of making bodies look as good as possible, of using wax and pipe cleaners to restore a face or making sure that a wig is on just right or that the embalming fluid is adequately distributed throughout the corpse.

The most frustrating part of the job, in fact, is dealing with relatives. "We try our best to please the family but sometimes the parent has cancer and the kids haven't seen them for a year or two and they don't realize how they deteriorate. They say, 'It doesn't even look like my mom.' Sometimes you work for hours on something and you can't get it to come out right. Like if someone's been in an accident and you're trying to restore the right side of the face, and the family wants it right there and then. "You never know what you're going to have in his job. Today we might have one case, tomorrow maybe seven. I might have an AIDS case, an accident case, a suicide case, might have a normal case, and they never take the same. You never embalm one person exactly the same as another."

Clark has difficulty embalming bodies that have undergone autopsies. "With autopsies you've got a lot of incisions to hide and if there are a lot of incisions, there's leakage." Autopsy cases usually take twice as long to embalm as individuals who have not been autopsied and there is a greater risk of infection to the embalmer.

Despite the many years he's spent doing it, Clark is not entirely enamored of embalming, primarily because he feels the pay is too low. "People think 'cause we're driving around in Cadillacs, we make a lot of money," he says. After seven years on the job, Clark makes roughly $2,000 a month. "I feel for the amount of time I'm putting in, safetywise, the cases I'm dealing with, I should get compensated more." Clark would like to leave embalming, though he plans to stick with the restorative and reconstructive process. "I've always wanted to do body and fender work," he says. And he firmly believes there's always the chance that Ed McMahon will pull his number. The day that happens, he says, he'll open up his own funeral home with first class service—a limo to pick up bodies, televisions for grieving families to watch and a compassionate payment plan that doesn't demand money up front.

For the moment, though, Clark will stick with embalming: "I'm a happy-go-lucky guy and I know somebody has to do this job."

Honolulu Weekly

PASSAGE B

Before You Listen

TASK 11

Of the three below, which person could possibly work at home and not have to travel to an office? Why?

A.

B.

C.

TASK 12

A program which would allow a government employee to work at home has many good points. Here are some advantages to talk about. What does each one mean?

1. allows for home care of children
2. cuts down on wear and tear of car
3. decreases traffic congestion
4. improves air quality
5. increases employee productivity
6. makes employees feel better
7. reduces traffic accidents
8. saves gasoline
9. saves money for parking costs
10. saves time

As You Listen

TASK 13

Listen to the news story. Circle each advantage mentioned above. Compare your answers with your classmates' answers.

After You Listen

TASK 14

Can you think of some other advantages? With a partner, write down as many as you can in complete sentences. Begin each sentence this way:

Staying at home and working *saves money on clothing*.

1. _____
2. _____
3. _____
4. _____
5. _____

Compare your sentences with your classmates' sentences.

TASK 15

Now read the following article about the news story you listened to. Look back at Chapter 1. What kind of family mentioned in that unit would this telecommuting plan be good for? Why? Write down your answer and reasons and present them to the rest of the class.

PASSAGE B

IT WORKS!
Learning Strategy:
Forming Concepts

Home work a blessing to staffers

Telecommuting plan draws praise

Kathy Oka used to leave her Waipio home at 5:45 a.m. heading downtown for work. Not anymore. With the use of a computer, modem and telephone—tools for telecommunication—Oka and Bernice Wong, who both work for the City Clerk's Office, have been able to work at home four days a week.

The city's Civil Service and Data Systems departments developed a workable telecommuting system that allows Oka and Wong to work at home.

The pilot program, designed to find out whether Oahu can cut traffic, save energy and diversify its work force by letting people work near their home, was started Sept. 1.

It is nearing its six-month review period.

City Clerk Raymond Pua said Oka and Wong report to their supervisors at Honolulu Hale and pick up a load of work once a week. Oka and Wong are regulated by deadlines. "We know when the work has to be done," Pua said.

The telecommuting workers like the arrangement.

"I beat the school jam," said Oka, a City Council aide whose primary responsibility is planning public hearings. Oka said she is only required to drive to City Hall once a week.

Most of Oka's work is clerical, such as typing agendas and contacting other city departments about public concerns. Because the work can be done on computer or over the phone, telecommuting is ideal for her, she said.

There's no need to deal with traffic and money saved on gas is another plus, Oka said. A single parent, Oka said the best part about working at home is spending more time with her 6-year-old son, Jayson.

"He and I have become closer," she said. The only negatives were the technical problems at the onset of the program, she said, but those are no longer a concern.

Wong, a Hawaii Kai resident, said working at home offers "a lot of flexibility."

A clerk for the Council Public Works and Safety Committee, Wong said working at home is "less stressful."

Telecommuting was a practical option for Wong, who at the start of the program was caring for her 2-month-old child. Wong said telecommuting allowed her to stay at home with her child rather than hire a babysitter.

At home, Wong handles phone calls, public inquiries and works on her computer. Wong also attends committee meetings during evening hours.

Wong said she completes her assignments in less time working at home because there's no opportunity to talk with other office workers. "It's more concentrated time," she said.

By Shannon Tangonan Advertiser Staff Writer

WORD STUDY

IT WORKS!
Learning Strategy:
Remembering New Material

TASK 16

The lecturer reported on a survey which ranked occupations. What other things is it possible to rank? Work together and make a list. How could these things be ranked? In terms of what? Based on what? Compare your answers with your classmates'.

THINGS THAT CAN BE RANKED	IN TERMS OF
1. <u>occupations</u>	<u>prestige</u>
2. <u>automobiles</u>	<u>size</u>

PASSAGE B

3. _____ _____
4. _____ _____
5. _____ _____
6. _____ _____
7. _____ _____
8. _____ _____
9. _____ _____
10. _____ _____

IT WORKS!
Learning Strategy:
Mapping

TASK 17

Look at the word map for *prestigious* things. Work with a partner and try to add as many words for things that are prestigious as you can.

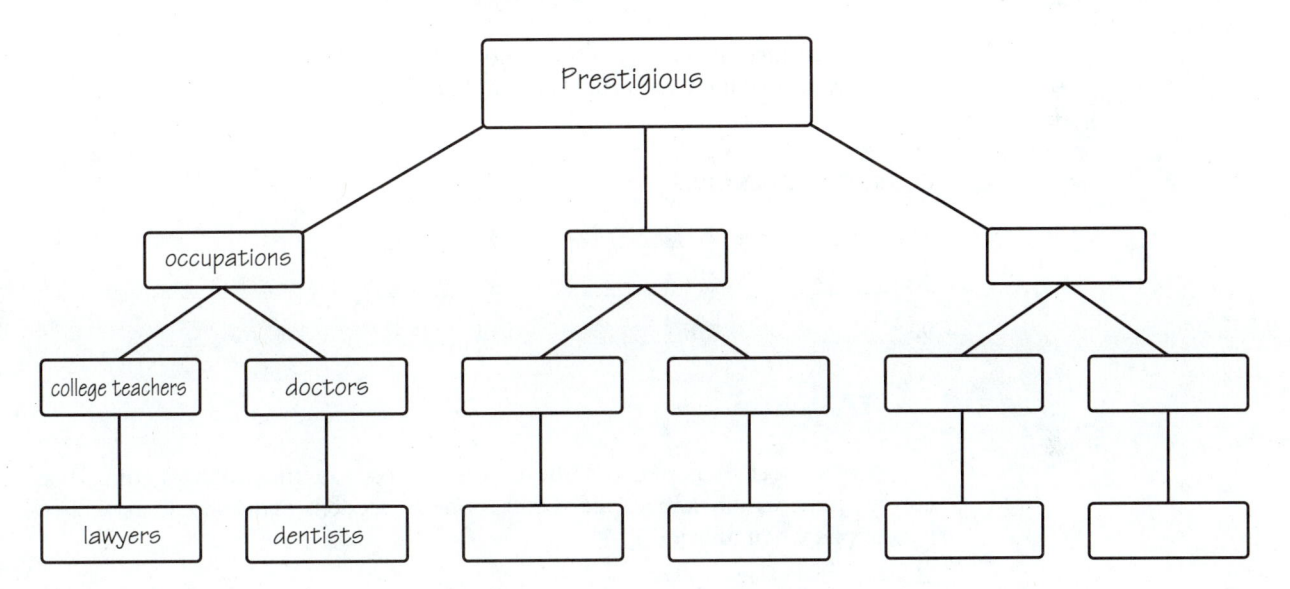

```
                    Prestigious
          /              |              \
   occupations           □               □
     /    \            /   \           /   \
college  doctors      □     □         □     □
teachers
   |       |
lawyers  dentists
```

Following Up

TASK 18

In groups of three or four, read the discussion suggestions and choose one to talk or write about. Afterwards, summarize discussion points and present them to the rest of the class. You could also read your paragraphs while your classmates listen and ask questions.

- Some people believe that Asian students are better in science and technical classes than Americans. Do you believe this? Why?
- What science/technical classes have you taken? Why did you take them? Do you feel everyone should take classes like these? Why?

CHAPTER 2 WORKING

Just for Fun

TASK 19

Get together with a partner and see how fast you can put the following story in correct order. Note down your time.

SCRAMBLED STORY: *"TWO BEERS"*

a. a few days later he came back
b. "and I wouldn't have to wash two glasses."
c. and the waitress said, "Two beers. Right?"
d. "My doctor told me to cut down on my drinking."
e. "No. One big glass."
f. "Say, why don't you order one big glass?"
g. the businessman didn't answer
h. the waitress always said, "Do you want the usual?"
i. "There's more beer in it"
j. this businessman always used to go to the same bar
k. "Yeah. Give me two small glasses of beer."

CORRECT SEQUENCE

1. _____ 2. _____ 3. _____ 4. _____
5. _____ 6. _____ 7. _____ 8. _____
9. _____ 10. _____ 11. _____ Time _____

TASK 20

On a sheet of paper, put the different pieces of the story together. Use correct punctuation and capital letters where needed. (You should have five paragraphs when finished.)

Threads

The largest union in America is the National Education Association (NEA) with 2 million members.

1992 Information Please Almanac, Houghton Mifflin Company

Name _____

Date _____

PASSAGE B

Now look at the following checklist of language learning strategies from Unit Two. How would you assess your progress in the use of each one? Use the following symbols:

S = **s**atisfied with progress
D = still **d**eveloping

Compare yours with the instructor's assessments.

LEARNING STRATEGY	MY ASSESSMENT	INSTRUCTOR'S ASSESSMENT
I am learning how to:	_____	_____
remember what I hear (remembering new material)	_____	_____
understand what I hear (forming concepts)	_____	_____
express myself even though I don't know all the words (remembering new material)	_____	_____
organize and assess what I hear and say (managing your learning)	_____	_____
speak and listen to others about personal feelings or views (understanding and using emotions)	_____	_____
earn with other people (understanding and using emotions)	_____	_____

Buying and Selling

CHAPTER 3

WHAT'S YOUR GOAL?

IT WORKS!
Learning Strategy:
Managing Your
Learning

Look at the following seven goals for Chapter 3. Which is the most important one for you? Mark it 1. How about the second most important? Mark it 2, etc.

I WANT TO LEARN HOW TO:	
A. remember what I hear	_____
B. understand what I hear	_____
C. guess the meaning of what I hear	_____
D. express myself even though I don't know all the words	_____
E. organize and assess what I hear and say	_____
F. speak and listen to others about personal feelings or views	_____
G. learn with other people	_____

THEME 1: PASSAGE A

Before You Listen

Americans use credit cards and buy things with credit more than any other people in the world. Find out about your classmates.

TASK 1

THEME 1: PASSAGE A

Write some questions to ask another person about credit cards. The first one is done for you.

1. Number of cards — How many credit cards do you have?
2. Name(s) of card(s) _____
3. Place(s) where card(s) came from (issuing agency) _____
4. Interest paid each month _____
5. Fee paid each year _____
6. Description of card(s) _____

*IT WORKS!
Learning Strategy:
Asking for
Clarification*

TASK 2

Find out who has credit cards in the class. Work with that person and ask the questions above. Write down the answers.

1. _____
2. _____
3. _____
4. _____
5. _____
6. _____

LEARNING STRATEGY

Forming Concepts: Summarizing helps learners understand better.

TASK 3

Write a summary of what you found out. Report your findings to the class. Use the following outline as a guide.

NAME has _____. The names of the cards are _____. The cards were issued by _____. Every month _____. Each year _____.

CHAPTER 3 BUYING AND SELLING

As You Listen

TASK 4

Now listen to the radio ad as many times as you want and fill in the necessary information to complete the chart. Compare answers with your classmates' answers.

NAME OF CARD _____

AGENCY _____

INTEREST _____

FEE _____

DESCRIPTION _____

THEME 1: PASSAGE B

Before You Listen

The Dolans are financial advisors on the radio who give advice to people who call in on the telephone. A man has called in about a problem with credit cards.

TASK 5

Look at the following list of questions. Which ones do you think the caller might ask the Dolans. Why?

1. How can I best use some money from a salary raise?
2. How can I build a swimming pool using credit?
3. How can I save money for my children's college education?
4. What can I do to make more money?
5. What can I do to reduce my monthly credit card payments?

TASK 6

Get together with a partner and make a list of some questions you think the caller might ask about credit cards.

POSSIBLE QUESTIONS

1. _____?
2. _____?
3. _____?
4. _____?
5. _____?

Threads

Lists of low-rate and no-fee credit card issuers are available for $1.50 each from Bankcard Holders of America, 560 Herndon Parkway, Suite 120, Herndon, VA 22070.

TASK 7

Look at the following situations. Talk about the ones that might describe the caller's situation.

SITUATION 1: The man's wallet with all his credit cards has been stolen. He wants to know what to do.
SITUATION 2: The man uses too much of his monthly income for credit card payments. He asks for advice.
SITUATION 3: The man wants to get a credit card. He does not know how.

As You Listen

TASK 8

Now listen to the first part of the conversation and see if your guesses were correct about the caller's situation and questions.

TASK 9

How do you think the Dolans will answer his question? Talk about the following possible answers.

ANSWER 1: Cut up all your credit cards and use only cash.
ANSWER 2: Invest the extra money in the stock market.
ANSWER 3: Use the extra money and pay off the credit card debt.

Now listen to the answer on the tape (the second part of the conversation) and see if you were correct.

TASK 10

What do you know about the <u>caller</u>? While listening again, look at the following list and circle the correct information. Talk about your answers.

Andrew	Ken
Married	Single
Own Home	Rent Home
4 children	3 children
$450 monthly credit payments	$350 monthly credit payments
Will get a salary raise	Will not get a salary raise

THEME 1: PASSAGE B

CHAPTER 3 BUYING AND SELLING

After You Listen

Word Study

TASK 11

Practice saying these words from the radio ad and the conversation. In a group of three or four, talk about what they mean.

balance	installment
blessed with	interest rate
debt	investment
homeowner	jump
income	strategy

TASK 12

Complete the following sentences by filling in the blanks with words from Task 11. Use each word only once. Be careful—sometimes word forms will change.

1. The majority of people in the United States are _____.
2. How many zeros are there in the national _____?
3. When buying things, many people use an _____ plan.
4. More people would borrow money if _____ were lower.
5. What _____ do you have for making money in the 90s?
6. Many elderly people live on a fixed _____.
7. She was lucky to get a _____ in her salary.
8. I bought the property as an _____ for the future.
9. He was _____ a talent for making money.
10. What is the _____ in your checking account?

TASK 13

Now look at the following word relationships. Fill in the blanks with the words from the list in Task 11. Talk about reasons for your answers.

1. *Find* is to *answer* as *plan* is to _____.
2. *Lend* is to *lender* as *invest* is to _____.
3. *Young* is to *old* as *renter* is to _____.
4. *Cook* is to *food* as *pay* is to _____.
5. *Female* is to *woman* as *payment* is to _____.

THEME 1: PASSAGE B

6. *Given* is to *gift* as _____ is to *salary raise*.
7. *Smoking* is to *cancer* as *overspending* is to _____.
8. *Soft* is to *loud* as *decrease* is to _____.
9. *Big* is to *large* as *salary* is to _____.
10. *Library* is to *book* as *credit card* is to _____.

TASK 14

IT WORKS!
Learning Strategy:
Remembering New
Material

Some of these words are from the listening passages. Look at each group and circle the word or phrase which does not belong. What are the reasons for your answers?

1. charges	debts	fees	payments
2. branch	company	office	outlet
3. American Express	Changing Times	Mastercard	Visa
4. CD	checking account	IRA	money market certificate
5. beyond control	in control	out of hand	out of control
6. a little more	a lot more	a touch more	slightly more
7. bucks	checks	plastic	wallets
8. built up	looked up	racked up	run up
9. advise	apply	recommend	suggest
10. a little bit of	during the course of	in the process	over time

Following Up

TASK 15

Read the discussion suggestions and choose one to talk or write about. After you finish, present your views to the rest of the class.

- Have you or a friend or relative had any bad personal experiences related to the use of credit cards? Tell what happened.
- In many countries and cultures, cash is preferred over credit cards. Why? How do you feel about that?

CHAPTER 3 BUYING AND SELLING

TASK 16

Mrs. Dolan suggested looking at a list of 800 numbers in *Changing Times* magazine for low interest rate credit cards. Here is that list. Call the numbers and see if the information is still current. Report your findings to the class.

Long-Term Winners

Which cards have the deepest roots in bargain territory?

▸ USAA (800-922-9092) has offered a low variable rate (recently 14.76%) and no annual fee since 1984. It's able to keep losses, and therefore costs, low because 95% of its 1.3 million cardholders are USAA members.

▸ People's Bank (800-423-3273; $25 annual fee for standard card. $40 for gold), of Bridgeport, Conn., has held its rate well below average since 1985 despite an increase from 13.5% to 13.9%.

▸ First Tennessee's gold card (800-234-2849; $35 annual fee) has been a bargain since 1985, even though the rate jumped from 12% to 14% last November.

▸ First Atlanta (800-241-7990; $25 standard, $40 gold; 14.88%) and Ohio Savings (800-356-1445; $18 standard, $30 gold; 14.75%) haven't raised their rates since 1986.

If you get hit with a rate hike, don't hesitate to switch cards. You can roll your balance onto a new, lower-rate card, but make sure you won't pay a higher cash-advance rate to do so. In some states, banks that raise rates must let you pay off your existing balance at the old rate, provided you don't use the card after the rate increase goes into effect.

TASK 17

The caller asked for help on how to control his debts. Look at the following worksheet and find out what your financial situation is. Are there other expenses that you have which are not listed? What are they? In groups of three or four, talk about the things you spend the most money for. Check with other groups to see if they are the same.

Achieving Credit Freedom

Bringing debts under control begins with calculating your state of indebtedness and coming up with a plan for slowly paying off your bills. A family with debts could use a worksheet like this to assess its financial status.

Step 1: Add up all income sources

Take-home pay (monthly)
Income from extra jobs
Spouse's take-home pay
Other income
Total

Step 2: Add up monthly living expenses

Phone
Power
Insurance
Bus fare
Union dues
Food
Clothing
Cleaning and laundry
Water
Gas and oil (car)
Rent or house payment
Child care
Donations
Child support
Medical-dental
Cable TV
Misc.
Total

Step 3: Total all debts

Bank charge cards
Department store charges
Car payments
Furniture payments, other debts
Total

Subtract monthly expenses from income. What remains is the amount that can be used to pay off debts.

Threads

On average, each American citizen owed 21% of his or her income in loans and credit card debt.

The Universal Almanac 1992, Andrews and McMeel.

IT WORKS!
Learning Strategy: Overcoming Limitations

TASK 18

Take a look at the following application for a credit card. Practice filling it in with a partner.

Please use ballpoint pen **Select One: Citibank Classic ☐ MasterCard® or ☐ Visa®**

PLEASE TELL US ABOUT YOURSELF

Print full name as you wish it to appear on the card. First, Middle, Last				
Your Home Address, Number and Street || Apt. No.	City or Town	State	Zip Code
Years at Current Address	☐ Own Home ☐ Own Condo/Co-op ☐ Rent ☐ Parents ☐ Other	Social Security Number	Date of Birth (Month/Day/Year)	
Home Phone and Area Code ( )		Name phone listed under		
Previous Home Address || Apt. No.	City or Town	State	Zip Code	Years There

PLEASE TELL US ABOUT YOUR JOB

Business Name or Employer	Position	Years At Job	Business Phone and Area Code ( )
Check Here If ☐ Retired ☐ Self-Employed	If Retired or Self-Employed, Bank Name	Bank Phone Number and Area Code ( )	Account Number

ABOUT YOUR INCOME

You need not include spouse's income, alimony, child support, or maintenance payments paid to you if you are not relying on them to establish creditworthiness. Your total **yearly** income from all sources must be at least $8,000 to be considered for cardmembership.

Your Total Personal **Yearly** Income	Other **Yearly** Household Income $
Source of Other **Yearly** Household Income	

ABOUT YOUR EXISTING ACCOUNTS

Please check those that apply. Be sure to specify Institution/Bank name.

☐ Money Market/NOW Account Institution Name:
☐ Checking Account Institution Name:
☐ Savings Account Institution Name:

WOULD YOU LIKE AN ADDITIONAL CARD AT NO CHARGE?

If yes, write in the full name of the user, First, Middle, Last

☐ Visa/MasterCard ☐ American Express Card ☐ Gasoline
☐ Diner's Club ☐ Department Store/Sears ☐ Other

PLEASE SIGN THIS AUTHORIZATION

By signing below I authorize Citibank (South Dakota), N.A. to check my credit history and exchange information about how I handle my account with proper persons, affiliates and credit bureaus if I am issued a card. I authorize my employer, my bank, and any other references listed above to release and/or verify information to Citibank (South Dakota), N.A. and its affiliates in order to determine my eligibility for the Citibank Classic card and any renewal or future extension of credit. If I ask, I will be told whether or not consumer reports on me were requested and the names of the credit bureaus with their addresses that provided the reports. If I designate any authorized users, credit bureaus may receive and report account information in the authorized users' name. I certify that I am 18 years of age, or older, and that the information provided is accurate. I understand that if I use the card or authorize its use or do not cancel my account within 30 days after I receive the card, the Citibank Agreement sent to me with the card will be binding on me. I have read and understand the disclosure box on the back. Terms and conditions are subject to change. **In order to be considered for a Citibank Classic card you must complete and sign this application. Omission of any of the information requested in this application may be grounds for denial.**

1B77S 0413D 2743L 0000

X _____
Applicant's Signature

Please allow 30 days to process your application. Do not send payment of $20 annual fee; you will be billed later. © Copyright 1991 Citibank (South Dakota) N.A.
Member F.D.I.C.

Date _____ Rev. 12/90

CITIBANK

THEME 2: PASSAGE A

Before You Listen

TASK 19

IT WORKS! Learning Strategy: Cooperating

Work together with a partner and make a list of both American (domestic) and foreign (imported) cars. You will have two minutes. Compare your lists with the rest of the class.

THEME 2: PASSAGE A

DOMESTIC	IMPORTED
1. _____	1. _____
2. _____	2. _____
3. _____	3. _____
4. _____	4. _____
5. _____	5. _____
6. _____	6. _____
7. _____	7. _____
8. _____	8. _____
9. _____	9. _____
10. _____	10. _____

TASK 20

Count the first 25 cars you see (parked in a parking lot, going by while you're on a street corner, etc.) How many are domestic? Imported? Compare your results with others. It is becoming more difficult to classify an automobile as either domestic or imported. Do you know why?

LEARNING STRATEGY

Forming Concepts: Guessing helps with overall language comprehension.

TASK 21

Of all the fifty states in the U.S., which one would you choose as being most representative of the whole nation for buying habits and preferences? Why?

As You Listen

TASK 22

Listen to the mini-lecture and see if your guess was correct.

CHAPTER 3 BUYING AND SELLING

IT WORKS!
Learning Strategy:
Forming Concepts

TASK 23

Look at the following sentences. Three have exactly the same meaning. Circle the three. How is the other sentence different?

1. In the future it is likely that the share of imports will go up.
2. It is most probable that the share of imports will increase in the future.
3. It is unknown whether the share of cars made outside the U.S. will increase.
4. The share of foreign-made cars will probably grow as time goes by.

TASK 24

The three sentences with the same meaning represent the main idea of the mini-lecture. Listen to the lecture again. Which of the three sentences uses the exact words you hear in the mini-lecture?

TASK 25

Look at the following graphs. They represent different information. Talk about what each one means.

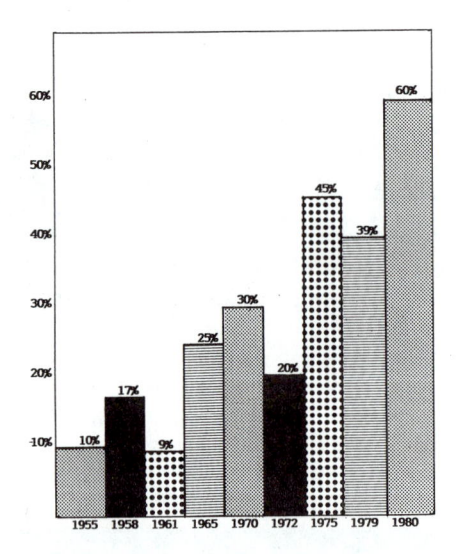

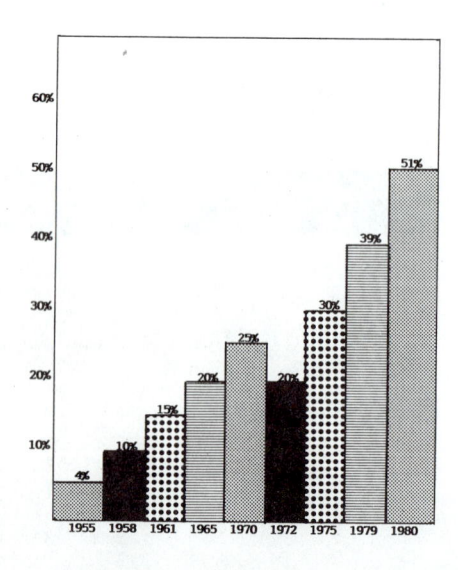

C.

[Bar graph showing percentages by year: 1955: 4%, 1958: 17%, 1961: 9%, 1965: 20%, 1970: 30%, 1972: 25%, 1975: 39%, 1979: 39%, 1980: 51%]

THEME 2: PASSAGE A

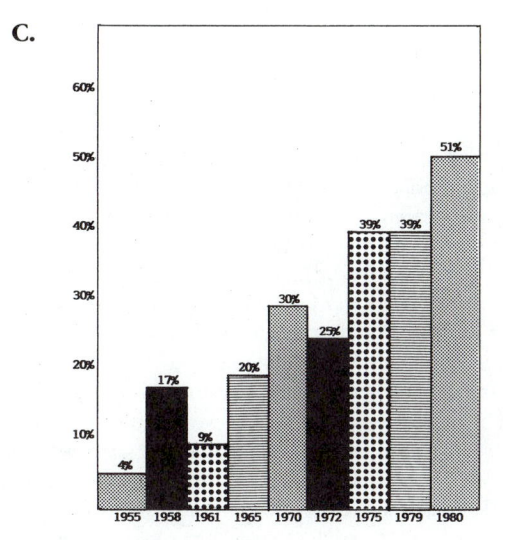

Threads

On February 15, 1972, Beetle No. 15,007,034 rolled off the assembly line, breaking the record set by the Ford Model T as the most produced automobile in history.

TASK 26

Now listen to the mini-lecture again. Choose the graph that represents what the speaker said.

After You Listen

TASK 27

The lecturer mentioned the popularity of Volkswagen automobiles in the U.S. Read the news story on page 52 about the Volkswagen. Talk and/or write about any part of the article which interests you. Summarize your feelings and report them to the rest of the class.

IT WORKS!
Learning Strategy:
Understanding and
Using Emotions

Beloved Beetle put-put-puts along

They say you can drive down any road in the world and chances are good a Volkswagen Beetle already has made the trip.

They also claim, these legions of Beetle fans, that the two most recognized shapes in the world are the hump-back Beetle and a Coke bottle.

With its put-put-put rear engine and a reputation for, of all things, floating, the 53-year-old Beetle distinguishes itself as the most produced car in automotive history. With almost 21 million Beetles manufactured to date, it surpasses the Model-T. (Henry Ford spewed out only a few more than 15 million of his legendary cars.)

An estimated 5 million Beetles were bought by U.S. consumers alone. And today, 14 years after its German manufacturer stopped mass production of the Beetle—it's now made and sold only in Mexico—an estimated $250,000 "bugs" still put-put on U.S. roads. Thousands of others reside in garages, undriven but adored.

Why this extended love affair for a car with a lousy heater, a battery stuck deep beneath the back seat, a body virtually unchanged for a half-century and the aerodynamics of an upright brick?

Owners sum it up this way: (A) It's cute. (B) It runs forever. (C) It's easy to fix, and (D) It's cute.

It's the kind of car people want to name. It's the kind of car that ends up in family scrapbooks.

Call it "the Cabbage Patch doll of the automotive world," says Donna Boland, manager of public relations for Volkswagen United States. "It's hardly great to look at. It's homely but endearing."

"I've heard people say they treat it like a member of the family who just happens to live in the garage," says Terry Shuler of Portage, Pa., president of the 2,000-member Vintage Volkswagen Club of America (VVCA). "I get letters from people wanting to find a good owner for an old VW."

Beetle owners want to talk, talk, talk about their Beetle.

They go on about how the little air-cooled engine always starts in cold weather. About its great gas mileage. About how the heavy-in-the-rear bug can beat a frontwheel drive car up an icy hill.

The Beetle's simplicity has endeared it to shade-tree mechanics.

The basic rule of thumb in VW care: Change the oil, often. (It takes pints, not quarts.)

A rebuilt VW engine can be had for about $500, and installing it is a snap, says Wally Elliott of Wyoming, who owns a 1974 gold Sunbug Beetle and just sold a 1972 Super Beetle—a variation of the bug made from 1971-'76—with 192,000 miles on it.

"Just four bolts you throw it in and off you go," he says. "It's like working on a toy. They are great cars—the only foreign car."

Tom Holmes of Akron, Ohio, sold Schultzy last year. There just wasn't enough garage room anymore at his house, nicknamed the "Old Volks Home," where he keeps three other vintage Beetles—a 1952, a '61 and a '69—plus a collection of 500 Volkswagen trinkets and models.

Volkslore surrounds us, from Herbie, the Love Bug, the star Beetle in four Walt Disney movies from 1969-80, to a Florida pest-control company with a fleet of bright yellow bugs customized with skinny black tails and round black ears to look like mice.

Year after year, Beetles looked the same—a "pregnant roller skate" was a popular description. Changes were subtle: The rear window, missing in early versions, grew gradually larger, bigger, elephant-foot taillights appeared in 1973; head restraints were added in 1968; double tailpipes gave way to a single pipe in 1975. There was an "automatic stick shift" version—heresy to most Beetles devotees—issued 1968-1976.

A Beetle could reach top speeds of 78-81 mph. It got 26 miles a gallon on regular gas, in the days before saving gas was important.

There were so many Beetles out there, it was bound to happen: Somehow, mothers started birthing babies in them. When the letters from proud parents started collecting, Volkswagen of America initiated its "Bonds for Babies Born in Beetles" campaign, offering a $50 savings bond to every documented Beetle birth.

The campaign continues today, expanded to cover births in any make of Volkswagen, Boland says.

Gannett News Service

THEME 2: PASSAGE A

TASK 28

Look at this ad from the newspaper. What does *pre-owned* mean? Can you think of another word that means the same thing? Which word is more commonly used by Americans? Which word sounds better to you? Why?

**WELL MAINTAINED & RELIABLE
PRE-OWNED 1990 COROLLA
& CAMRY 4-DOOR SEDANS
WITH REMAINING FACTORY WARRANTIES!**

(Lic. DCY-338)   (Lic. MSP-232)

'90 CAMRY 4-DOOR SEDAN **$10,495***

'90 COROLLA 4-DOOR SEDAN **$8,495***

Automatic, Power Steering, Air Conditioning, AM/FM Stereo

*IT WORKS!
Learning Strategy:
Understanding and
Using Emotions*

TASK 29

It is common for Americans to buy pre-owned things. What about in your country? Talk about what people do with items no longer needed or wanted. How do you feel about this?

LEARNING STRATEGY

Remember New Material: Marking important material helps you remember them.

TASK 30

Marking important ideas helps you remember them. Take a look at this article on how to buy a car on page 54. Highlight important suggestions listed. Then, with a partner, talk and/or write about them

How to buy a used car that works

So there you are. Stranded by the side of the road. Smoke is pouring out from under the hood while traffic breezes by. The used car expiring in front of you looked like a good deal when you bought it. Now it looks like a nightmare.

Take this column with you when you go shopping for a used car.

The first order of business is to decide what kind of used car you want. Go to the library and do a little research. *Consumer Reports* publishes an auto issue every April; in it, you will find valuable tips on what to look for when you're shopping for a used car. The report also lists recommended used cars and cars to avoid. *Consumer Reports* also publishes an annual *Used Cars Buying Guide*. While you're at the library, also take a look at the *National Automobile Dealers Association (NADA) Official Used Car Guide*. This monthly report gives retail and wholesale list prices for automobiles that are up to 6 years old. While you're researching, give the Better Business bureau a call and get a copy of their brochure *Tips On Buying A Used Car*. When you decide what kind of car you want, set a budget that takes into account the price you can afford, including tax, registration and insurance.

Now you're ready to go shopping. Take along a friend who has some mechanical knowledge to lend a hand inspecting cars. If you don't know anyone with mechanical skills, take someone whose judgment you trust.

Where you buy your car invariably influences what you get and how much you pay for it. New car dealerships usually sell cars that have been traded int. Their prices tend to be higher, to compensate for overhead. Before doing business with a dealer, check with the Better Business Bureau and the Regulated Industries Complaint Office to see if any complaints have been filed against them.

(Remember that all used cars are sold "as is" unless a warranty is included in the transaction. Car dealerships are required by law to post warranty information on the car's window.)

Used car lots can be cheaper than new car lots, but you have to be careful. An old, run-down car can look like a million bucks with a new paint job. Don't shop at night, and don't take a dealer's word on a car's reliability. Take the car to an independent mechanic you trust. If you don't know one, ask a friend or call the American Automobile Association for a referral.

While you're driving to the mechanic's, take the time to inspect the car yourself. Was there spot on the ground under the car that might indicate an oil leak? How does the car handle? Does it pull to one side? Is the ride smooth or bumpy? Do the brakes squeak? Is the interior in good shape? Pull over and have your friend check as you signal for a turn and hit the brakes. Do the lights work? Is there an unusual amount of smoke coming from the tail pipe? Have your friend keep notes, and ask the mechanic to check out any questionable areas.

If you do decide to buy a used car from a dealer, get all the details of the transaction. If you have any questions, include them in the contract. Make sure you know what the warranty covers. Never leave any blank spaces in a contract. Read it carefully before you sign it—once you sign the contract and drive off the lot, the car is your responsibility.

If the dealers are beyond your budget, take a look in the newspaper. Cars sold by private parties are usually cheaper since there's no overhead involved. With these cars, what you see is what you get. Remember that the seller's advertised price is usually what they hope to get. Don't hesitate to negotiate before making an offer. Once again, take the car on a test drive to your trusty mechanic. And if you guy a car this way, make sure you get the title and registration with the seller's signature that releases the car to you.

While looking through the newspaper, you might come across ads for companies offering to put you in touch with car owners that can't make their loan payments. BEWARE! These "auto equity" promotions have caused problems, and they're better left alone. Give the Better Business Bureau a call for their brochure *Tips On Auto Equity Promotions* if you want more information.

Chris Brennan

Word Study

THEME 2: PASSAGE A

> **LEARNING STRATEGY**
>
> **Remembering New Material:** Assigning vocabulary words to different word groups is a good way to remember them.

TASK 31

Look at these "movement" words found in the mini-lecture. Practice saying them. Talk about their meanings with a partner.

____ 1. catch up

____ 2. fluctuation

____ 3. runs ahead

____ 4. rolled around

____ 5. slight dip

____ 6. steady decline

____ 7. steady rise

____ 8. upsurge

TASK 32

Make a list of other movement words you can think of. Write them on the lines.

____ 9. _____

____ 10. _____

____ 11. _____

____ 12. _____

____ 13. _____

____ 14. _____

____ 15. _____

CHAPTER 3 BUYING AND SELLING

TASK 33

Now mark each item in tasks 31 and 32 according to the direction of its movement. Use the following symbols:

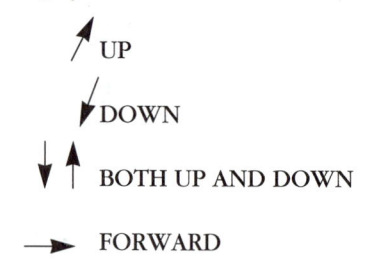

↗ UP

↘ DOWN

↓↑ BOTH UP AND DOWN

→ FORWARD

Talk about your answers and reasons for marking the words as you did.

IT WORKS!
Learning Strategy:
Remembering New Material

TASK 34

Complete the following sentences by filling in the blanks with words from the list in Task 31.

1. After a certain age, most people experience a _____ in health.

2. If we don't run a little faster, the other joggers will _____ for sure.

3. Last night the weather was cold. Today it is warm. There has been a huge _____ in temperature.

4. Our class usually _____ of all the others in the entire school.

5. The Christmas season has _____ too soon this year.

6. There will have to be a quick _____ of support if she wants to win the election.

7. The news is good. Economists are predicting a _____ in the economy next year.

8. The news is not good. Economists are predicting a _____ in the economy next year.

THEME 2: PASSAGE B

Before You Listen

IT WORKS!
Learning Strategy:
Forming Concepts

TASK 35

Look at the following illustrations. What items are being advertised? Where are they being advertised? Why would advertisers *not* advertise the items in the ways that they are shown?

THEME 2: PASSAGE B

A.

B.

C.

D.

E.

TASK 36

If you were an advertiser, where would you advertise the products above? Why?

CHAPTER 3 BUYING AND SELLING

TASK 37

Advertisers divide up the population according to age groups. Work together with a partner and figure out five different age categories. What would you call each one? What percentage of the total population would each one be?

AGE	NAME	PERCENTAGE
1. _____	_____	_____
2. _____	_____	_____
3. _____	_____	_____
4. _____	_____	_____
5. _____	_____	_____

IT WORKS!
Learning Strategy:
Taking Notes

As You Listen

TASK 38

Listen to the mini-lecture. Take notes and compare your lecture notes with your work above. Use abbreviations or symbols if you can.

AGE	NAME	PERCENTAGE
1. _____	_____	_____
2. _____	_____	_____
3. _____	_____	_____
4. _____	_____	_____
5. _____	_____	_____

Threads

An estimated $132.6 billion was spent on advertising in the United States in 1990.

McCann-Erickson, New York

After You Listen

IT WORKS!
Learning Strategy:
Understanding and Using Emotions

TASK 39

Read the following short news article. Would people in your country be interested in these unusual products? How about in the United States?

THEME 2: PASSAGE B

> ## Some Japan products a little unusual
>
> TOKYO—Along with high-tech goods like cellular phones, Japan's hottest products this year include pantyhose that block out harmful sun rays and a hangover remedy, "Go For It, Mr. Liver!"
>
> The potion, one of a number of fast-sellers aimed at Japan's heavy-drinking businessmen, more than doubled expected sales projections, said an annual survey published by Japan's largest ad agency.
>
> Another top-selling item, a liquor-based cocktail called "Green Banana Fizz," probably caused some of the hangovers. Millions of bottles were imbibed this year, Dentsu Inc. said.

TASK 40

Talk and/or write about any unusual products you have seen or heard about in the U.S. or some other country.

TASK 41

Talk and/or write about the following questions:

- Where would advertisers advertise the above items? Why?
- What age group would buy these products? Why?

TASK 42

Read the following newspaper article about advertisers and "grumpies." Do the following:

1. Highlight the meaning of "grumpie."
2. Identify the age group from the mini-lecture that "grumpies" belong in.
3. Highlight examples of products being promoted by advertisers for "grumpies."
4. Talk and/or write about any of these products.

Threads

Nine million video cassettes of *The Little Mermaid* were sold in the United States in 1990.

Video Store, 1991.

Advertisers taking aim at the grumpies

Graying baby boomers a potential gold mine for firms

For the first time since they began arriving after World War II, the 78 million Americans of the baby boom are being courted by large numbers of marketers, not for their seemingly endless youth but for their encroaching middle age.

As the baby boomers begin to bulge, sag and squint their way into their mid-40s, companies are striking gold with products that offer a bit of youth to these aging yuppies—a group that demographers are calling grumpies, for grown-up mature professionals.

Retailers are ringing up profits with products like wide-seated jeans, frilly girdles and expensive bifocals without telltale lines in the lenses.

This month, in several states, RJR Nabisco introduced miniature Oreos intended to give baby boomers a taste from childhood without adding to their anxieties over their waistlines.

Haagen-Dazs recently added a smaller ice-cream bar.

And this month, the makers of Lee's jeans began a multimillion-dollar advertising campaign aimed at jeans wearers with youthful hearts but expanding behinds.

Driving such innovations, analysts say, is a belief that the success of many products in the 1990s will depend on how well they adapt to a great transition in the population, as Americans born between 1946 and 1964 move into their middle years.

In a sense, the makers and marketers of consumer products say they will have to make the transition more gracefully than the grumpies, the most affluent baby boomers, who have shown signs of fighting middle age every step of the way.

"You have a lot of people who have been nurtured, groomed, coddled and almost brainwashed to think of themselves as youthful," said Jeff Ostroff, director of Primelife Marketing, a group in Plymouth Meeting, Pa., that advises marketers who want to reach older consumers.

"To maintain that perception as the with-it generation, this group of people will fight."

The graying of the baby boomers will affect nearly every aspect of society, from housing to medical care to the nation's savings rates.

But nowhere is the impact more visible than in the world of consumer products, where this generation, because of its disproportionate size, has commanded the attention of companies since the days of the Hula-Hoop and the Davy Crockett cap.

In the $7 billion jeans industry, for example, Lee Apparel Co.'s new advertising campaign began on Aug. 2, with television commercials showing men struggling to pull on their old jeans.

It uses slogans like: "Forget about cholesterol. It's your jeans that have been cutting off your circulation."

For years, jeans makers sold more than half of their products to consumers 14 to 24 years old, and the companies' advertising was crowded with young, slim models.

But now, more than 60 percent of jeans buyers are over 25 and Levi Strauss & Co. has sharply increased its market share with "relaxed fit" jeans aimed at people in their 30s and 40s.

As the most affluent fraction of the baby-boom generation, grumpies are the favorite target for many marketers.

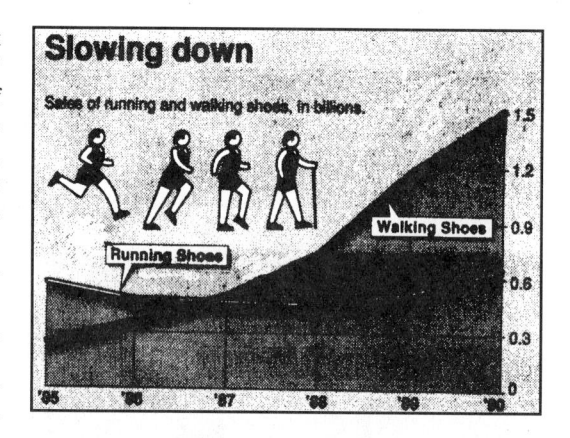

Opticians, for example, report a rising market in lineless bifocal glasses, camouflage for a sign of middle age.

Even though the lenses cost twice as much as the standard bifocals with the lines, sales to new customers jumped more than 50 percent in the last two years.

"When the doctor said I needed bifocals, I thought: 'No way!'" said Linda Sterling, an engineer from Plainsboro, N.J., who discovered lineless bifocals and leaped to pay $300 for a pair in Ralph Lauren frames. "I refuse to get old. I just will not get old. Age is just a mindset."

Sterling declined to disclose her age other than to say she was born shortly after World War II.

Despite creaking knees and aching backs, many running buffs of a decade ago are still buying shoes on the cutting edge of technology—even for exercise that now rarely takes them faster than four miles an hour.

Last year, sales of walking shoes in the United States topped $1.5 billion, twice the dollar sales of running shoes, National Sporting Goods Association said.

New York Times

Name _____

Date _____

THEME 2: PASSAGE B

    Now look at the following checklist of language learning strategies from Unit Three. How would you assess your progress in the use of each one? Use the following symbols:

    S = satisfied with progress

    D = still developing

    Compare yours with the instructor's assessments.

LEARNING STRATEGY	MY ASSESSMENT	INSTRUCTOR'S ASSESSMENT
I am learning how to:		
remember what I hear (placing words, associating, grouping)	_____	_____
understand what I hear (analyzing, highlighting, reasoning, summarizing)	_____	_____
guess the meaning of what I hear (guessing)	_____	_____
express myself even though I don't know all the words (taking notes, practicing)	_____	_____
organize and assess what I hear and say (paying attention)	_____	_____
speak and listen to others about personal feelings or views (discussing feelings)	_____	_____
learn with other people (cooperating, developing cultural understanding)	_____	_____

Keeping Healthy

CHAPTER 4

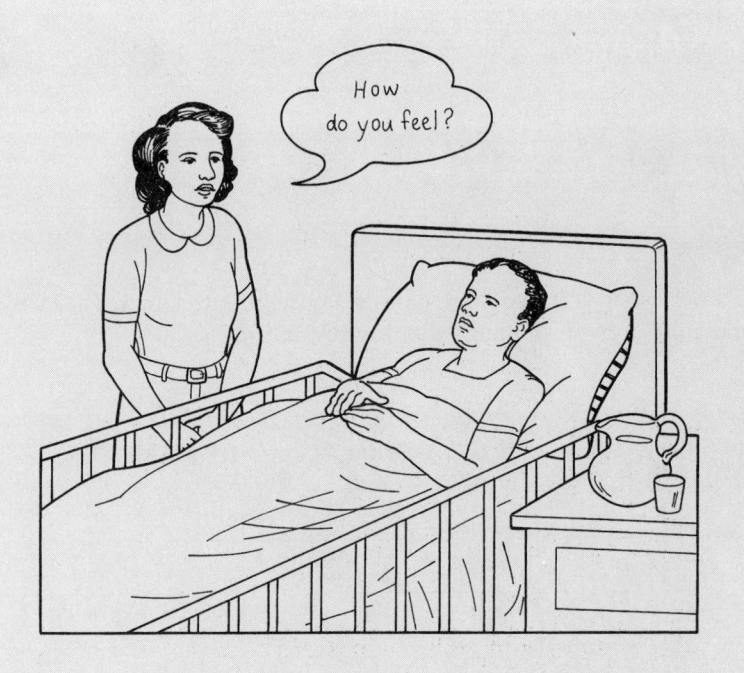

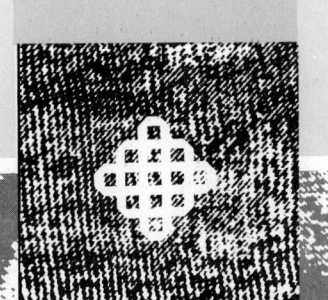

WHAT'S YOUR GOAL?

Look at the following five goals for Chapter 4. Which is the most important one for you? Mark it 1. How about the second most important? Mark it 2, etc.

IT WORKS!
Learning Strategy:
Managing Your Learning

I WANT TO LEARN HOW TO:	
A. remember what I hear	____
B. understand what I hear	____
C. guess the meaning of what I hear	____
D. speak and listen to others about personal feelings or views	____
E. learn with other people	____

PASSAGE A

Before You Listen

IT WORKS!
Learning Strategy:
Cooperating

TASK 1

Find out what you and your partner know about cancer. Fill in the chart below and compare your findings with the rest of the class.

KINDS OF CANCER	HOW DIAGNOSED	HOW TREATED
_____	_____	_____
_____	_____	_____
_____	_____	_____
_____	_____	_____
_____	_____	_____
_____	_____	_____

TASK 2

Read the following newspaper article.

PASSAGE A

IT WORKS!
Learning Strategy:
Forming Concepts

Mammogram still underused tool

The number of women who have had at least one mammogram has risen sharply over the past several years, but the majority are still not getting breast x-rays as often as they should, according to a 1990 survey by the Jacobs Institute of Women's Health and the National Cancer Institute.

Breast cancer is second only to lung cancer as the leading cause of cancer death in women. Studies indicate that mammography is the most effective method for detecting breast cancer in its earliest and most curable stages.

Without looking at a dictionary, what is the definition of a mammogram?

LEARNING STRATEGY

Understanding and Using Emotions: Becoming aware of others' thoughts and feelings helps you understand yourself and others.

TASK 3

Read the following statements. In pairs or small groups talk about why you think each statement is true or false. What are the reasons for your answers?

1. One out of five women in Hawaii gets breast cancer.
2. One out of nine women in America gets breast cancer
3. Some women can get mammograms at their workplaces.
4. "Mammovans" are vehicles equipped to take breast x-rays.
5. Companies can save money by allowing employees to get mammograms.
6. Some women can get mammograms at hospitals.
7. It takes a long time to get a mammogram.

As You Listen

TASK 4

Now listen to the news story about mammograms. Are the statements in Task 3 true, false, or maybe both. Why?

LEARNING STRATEGY

Forming Concepts: Analyzing information and applying it helps you to understand it better.

TASK 5

Look at the following flyer. Complete the ad by filling in the blanks. You can listen to the news story again.

> **MAMMOGRAPHY AT THE MALL**
>
> Every _____(1), Castle Hospital's mammography _____(2) makes an appearance at a major shopping _____(3) around the county. Castle technicians perform _____(4) from 10 a.m. to 5:45 at each site. The screening process takes _____(5) minutes per person. Call the _____(6) on-the-move office (555-3105) to schedule an appointment.

Threads

To find an accredited mammography center, call the National Cancer Institute (800/4-CANCER).

PASSAGE A

After You Listen

Following Up

TASK 6

Look at the following newspaper article and accompanying graphs about breast cancer in the U.S. According to the article, what kind of people are at risk for getting the disease? Highlight that information.

Breast Cancer in the U.S.

Breast cancer is the cancer most commonly diagnosed in women, and kills more than any but lung cancer. Last year, it killed 300 men and 44,000 women, striking a body part at once intimate and obvious, sexual and maternal, one that more than any other symbolizes femininity.

In 1940, 1 in 20 American women got the disease in their lifetimes. Today, it is estimated that 1 in 9 women will. Better detection through wider mammography screening explains the rapid increase in the last decade, but not the longer trend. Some women want it declared an epidemic.

"Five women are dying every hour of this disease," says Virginia Soffa, 40, who in February founded the Breast Cancer Action Group in Burlington, Vt. "If there was a mass murderer killing five women every hour we would be doing a heck of a lot more."

They are angry that the number of women stricken by the disease keeps rising, that there remains no known cause or cure.

The experts have theories. A family history of breast cancer increases a woman's chances of getting the disease. So does having children after the age of 30, or never having children. So do early menstruation or late menopause, obesity or being over the age of 50. Oral contraceptives or estrogen replacement may increase the odds. Perhaps the greatest risk is a high-fat diet.

But any woman who attempts to calculate her risks and alter her lifestyle accordingly must consider this number: Almost 60 percent of women who get breast cancer have no obvious risk factors.

The first step toward solving the puzzle, the activists say, is simple: spend more money. Breast cancer activists contend that the federal government spends too little on the disease, and too much of what it does spend supports tired approaches to surgery, radiation and chemotherapy—treatments they have dubbed "slash, burn and poison." More is needed, they say, for innovative therapies and basic research into the possible cause of the disease.

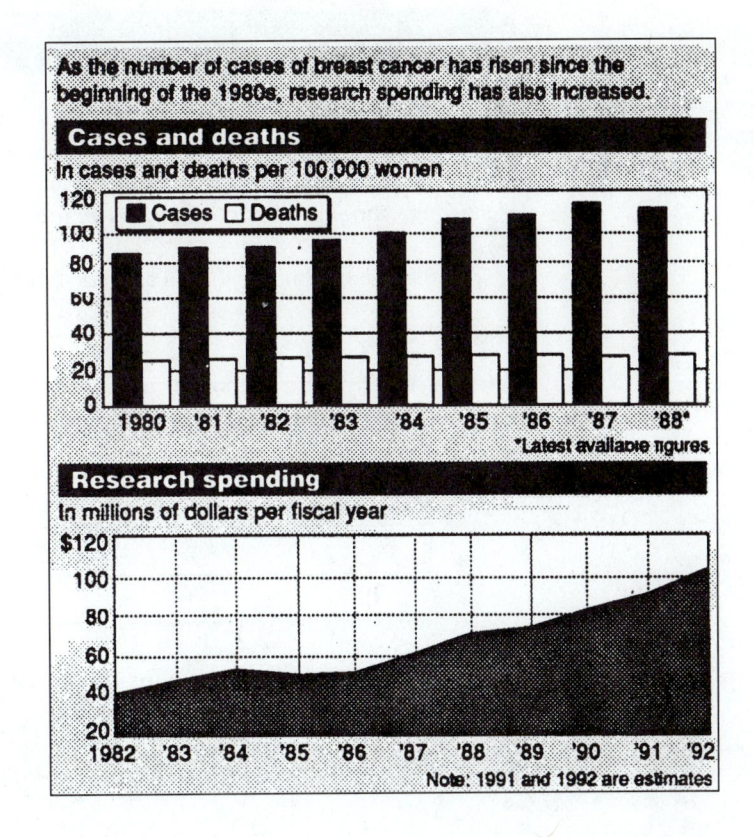

As the number of cases of breast cancer has risen since the beginning of the 1980s, research spending has also increased.

Cases and deaths
In cases and deaths per 100,000 women

■ Cases □ Deaths

1980 '81 '82 '83 '84 '85 '86 '87 '88*
*Latest available figures

Research spending
In millions of dollars per fiscal year

1982 '83 '84 '85 '86 '87 '88 '89 '90 '91 '92
Note: 1991 and 1992 are estimates

CHAPTER 4 KEEPING HEALTHY

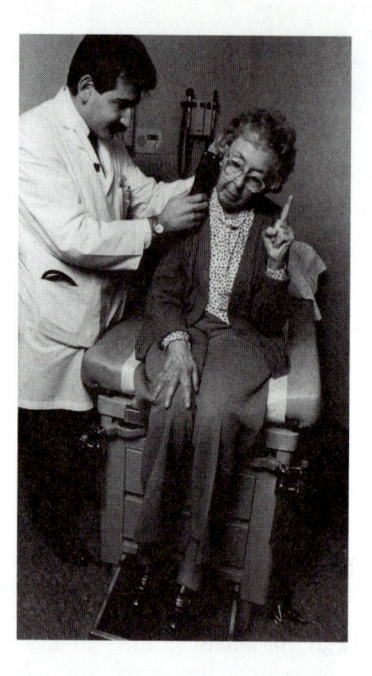

TASK 7

Breast cancer is primarily a women's disease. What other "women's diseases" are there? Are there also "men's diseases"? Talk or write about any personal experiences related to these diseases. Summarize your thoughts and present them to the rest of the class.

PASSAGE B

*IT WORKS!
Learning Strategy:
Understanding and
Using Emotions*

Before You Listen

TASK 8

Work with a partner and talk about what a child *should* and *must* do before starting school in your country. Write four sentences.

1. Before beginning school a child should
   _____

2. _____
   _____

3. Before beginning school a child must
   _____

4. _____
   _____

Are all of the above true for children in the United States also?

PASSAGE B

TASK 9

Look at the following words. Which one does not belong? Why?

cancer	influenza	mumps
chicken pox	measles	polio

TASK 10

Look at the following headlines from a newspaper. In pairs or a small group change each headline to a complete sentence. Compare sentences with classmates. (Note: HI is the postal abbreviation for Hawaii.)

1. Shots Required—HI Preschoolers
   _____
   _____

2. John Lewin—State Health Director
   _____
   _____

3. Lewin: Free Mass Immunizations All HI Residences
   _____
   _____

4. 17th Pacific Science Congress in Waikiki
   _____
   _____

> **Threads**
>
> The Centers for Disease Control have a list of vaccinations and inoculations needed when visiting foreign countries. Call 404/332-4559 for information.

As You Listen

TASK 11

Now listen to the news story. Choose the main idea from the four sentences above.

After You Listen

TASK 12

Before coming to the United States, everyone was probably required to have certain immunizations. Talk about the shots you had.

CHAPTER 4 KEEPING HEALTHY

TASK 13

Read the following descriptions of diseases everyone should know about. Which ones have you been vaccinated against?

4 DISEASES EVERYONE SHOULD KNOW ABOUT

MEASLES
(also called "rubeola") is a serious threat to young adults. Millions of young people still haven't been immunized. Others born between 1957-1968 may have received an ineffective vaccine.

SYMPTOMS INCLUDE:
- high fever
- rash
- watery eyes
- runny nose
- cough
- other signs of a "cold."

POSSIBLE COMPLICATIONS
- pneumonia
- encephalitis (inflammation of the brain)
- ear infection (possibly leading to deafness)
- early labor or miscarriage, if contracted by a pregnant woman
- death.

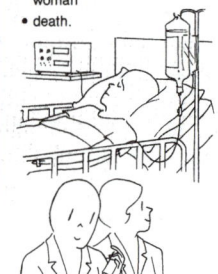

RUBELLA
(also called "German measles") is very contagious. It can be spread to others before the infected person has symptoms.

SYMPTOMS INCLUDE:
- rash on face and neck (sometimes mild)
- swelling in neck
- aching muscles
- headache
- slight fever.

POSSIBLE COMPLICATIONS
for a pregnant woman who contracts rubella include having:
- a miscarriage
- a stillborn baby
- a baby with serious birth defects.

Note: If you're pregnant or planning to become pregnant within the next 3 months, you should not receive the rubella vaccine. Wait until after you've had your baby.

"MMR" is a vaccine that gives lifetime protection against measles, mumps and rubella -- 3 in 1!

TETANUS
(also called "lockjaw") is caused by getting contaminated dirt in a burn, wound, scratch or other break in the skin. These injuries often occur around the home or yard.

SYMPTOMS:
Stiffness builds in the jaw and face, progressing to the back and abdomen. Additional symptoms include:
- pain while chewing
- weakness
- tiredness
- headache
- fever.

POSSIBLE COMPLICATIONS:
- heart problems
- difficulty breathing
- death.

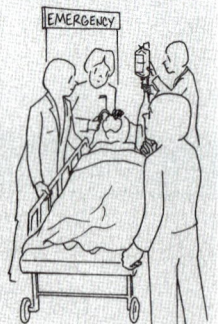

DIPHTHERIA
used to be the cause of serious epidemics. Now it can be controlled with vaccines.

SYMPTOMS INCLUDE:
- chills
- slight fever
- severe sore throat
- gray coating on tongue.

POSSIBLE COMPLICATIONS:
- blocked windpipe
- heart failure
- inflammation of nerves and lining of the heart
- death.

A "Td" shot will protect you from both tetanus and diphtheria. A booster shot every 10 years is necessary.

PASSAGE B

TASK 14

One of the most common immunizations given these days is a flu shot. Read the following news article. Find out when is the best time for getting a flu shot.

What you're sick with is probably not flu—not yet

If you have a raspy voice and a runny nose today, relax. The flu season has not arrived ahead of schedule. What you probably are suffering from is para-influenza or a rhinovirus or an enterovirus, which somewhat mimic symptoms of the real flu, or influenza, but do not pack the same wallop.

While the copycat ailments can be uncomfortable and something of a nuisance for a few days, unlike influenza, they simply do not develop into pneumonia, which in many cases leads to death, experts say.

"The only thing to help prevent the flu is to get a shot," said Dr. Joanna Buffington, a physician in the flu branch of the Center for Disease Control in Atlanta.

"People seem to be afraid of adverse reactions," she said. "But let me tell you, the most common side effect is a sore arm and the second, which is not very common, is a slight fever.

"The vaccine is a killed virus strain so that it is no longer capable of causing infection but it still holds on to its immune system-stimulating properties, which is why it works to prevent infection from the live virus."

Buffington stressed that the boost to the immune system takes about two weeks to work. Often, however, a person has not gotten a flu shot by January and then discovers everyone in his office has influenza, so he rushes out and gets a shot. Then, the next day in the office someone coughs on him and he soon comes down with the flu.

"Then, that person is apt to say, 'The shot didn't work' or 'The shot gave me the flu,'" she said. "But, actually, they didn't get the shot in time. They were exposed to influenza and were infected before the shot had a chance to work."

The time frame for influenza shots is October and November, and, "unfortunately for us in the business, October and November are peak seasons for other viruses, like para-influenza, a virus that causes respiratory, coldlike symptoms; hundreds of rhinoviruses, which cause the common cold, or many entero viruses, which like influenza, cause headaches and muscle aches."

"The problem is that a lot of people call anything flu," Buffington said. "But influenza is a very specific virus."

Influenza usually strikes suddenly and produces fever—and it can cause a pretty good fever, as well as muscle aches, fatigue and a dry, hacking cough, she said.

The ideal time for flu shots is long before the appearance, usually in December, of the first cases. Glezon suggests being vaccinated by Thanksgiving at the latest.

Word Study

TASK 15

Look at these six nouns taken from the listening passages. Without using a dictionary, in groups of three or four, talk about what each one means. Practice saying them.

_____ 1. immunization

_____ 2. shopping mall

_____ 3. lawmakers

_____ 4. legislation

_____ 5. vaccine

_____ 6. worksites

LEARNING STRATEGY

Remembering New Material: Assigning vocabulary words to different word groups is a good way to remember them.

*IT WORKS!
Learning Strategy:
Remembering New Material*

TASK 16

Work with a partner and classify each word in task 15. Is the word used in business (B), government (G), or health (H)? Why?

TASK 17

Look at the following groups of words. Cross out the item that does not belong with the other three. Talk about reasons for your answers.

1. immunization   shot   vaccination   x-ray
2. shopping center   shopping list   shopping mall   shopping plaza
3. doctors   lawmakers   legislators   representatives
4. guidelines   laws   legislation   regulations
5. aspirin   flu shot   prescription drug   vaccine
6. factories   offices   schools   worksites

TASK 18

Look at these six verbs taken from the listening passages. Without using a dictionary, in groups of three or four, talk about what each one means. Practice saying them.

_____ 1. diagnosed

_____ 2. estimates

_____ 3. equipped with

_____ 4. invested

_____ 5. lobby

_____ 6. vaccinated

Work with a partner and classify each word. Is the word used in business (B), government (G), or health (H)? Why?

Threads

Acupuncture, founded thousands of years ago in China, is the oldest medicine practiced today.

TASK 19

Look at the groups of words below. Cross out the item that does not belong with the other three. Talk about reasons for your answers.

1. determined   diagnosed   found out   operated
2. estimates   says   guesses   predicts
3. equipped with provided with registered with supplied with
4. bought   invested   sold   spent
5. lobby   request   urge   utilize
6. got shots   got x-rays   immunized   vaccinated

Following Up

TASK 20

Read the discussion suggestions and choose one to talk or write about. After you finish, present your views to the rest of the class.

- Thanks to recent scientific and technological advances, early diagnosis of serious illnesses can be made. Besides the x-ray, what other discoveries have helped find the presence of disease in the human body?
- There is great hope that science will discover a vaccine so human beings can be immunized against the HIV virus which causes AIDS. Do you think this will happen in the near future? Why? What other diseases would you like to see vaccines for?

Just for Fun

TASK 21

What does "leading a healthy life" mean to you? What kinds of things would you do if you wanted to lead a healthy life? What kinds of things would you not do?

- Form groups of ten or fewer. If there are fifteen members in the class, break up into groups of eight and seven, and so forth.
- Your instructor will give each of you a strip of paper with a sentence or phrase on it. The words make up a story about a girl named Diane. Read the words and memorize them. Don't show your words to anyone. Don't write down the words.
- The instructor will collect the strips. Now work together and try to combine the sentences and phrases into the complete story. Use only your listening and speaking abilities.

After you finish Chapter 4, go to the appendix section at the end of this text and begin Each One/Teach One.

PASSAGE B

Threads

For more information about AIDS, call the National Centers for Disease Control's AIDS Hot Line, 24-hours a day at 800/342-AIDS.

*IT WORKS!
Learning Strategy:
Understanding and
Using Emotions*

Threads

Different people need different amounts of sleep. Albert Einstein needed 10 hours of sleep a night, but Thomas Edison needed only four or five.

CHAPTER 4 KEEPING HEALTHY

Name _____

Date _____

Now look at the following checklist of language learning strategies from Chapter 4. How would you assess your progress in the use of each one? Use the following symbols:

S = satisfied with progress

D = still developing

Compare yours with the instructor's assessments.

LEARNING STRATEGY	MY ASSESSMENT	INSTRUCTOR'S ASSESSMENT
I am learning how to:		
remember what I hear (remembering new material)	_____	_____
understand what I hear (forming concepts)	_____	_____
guess the meaning of what I hear (forming concepts)	_____	_____
speak and listen to others about personal feelings or views (understanding and using emotions)	_____	_____
learn with other people (understanding and using emotions)	_____	_____

Thinking about Feelings

CHAPTER 5

WHAT'S YOUR GOAL?

Look at the following six goals for Chapter 5. Which is the most important one for you? Mark it 1. How about the second most important? Mark it 2, etc.

IT WORKS!
Learning Strategy:
Managing Your
Learning

I WANT TO LEARN HOW TO:	
A. remember what I hear	____
B. understand what I hear	____
C. express myself even though I don't know all the words	____
D. organize and assess what I hear and say	____
E. speak and listen to others about personal feelings or views	____
F. learn with other people	____

PASSAGE A

Before You Listen

TASK 1

Following is a list of nine adjectives that describe how people feel. Practice saying them. Following the list of words, there are nine definitions. Write the correct word in the space in its definitions. Check your answers with classmates.

>   annoyed   embarrassed   neutral
>   bored   excited   pleased
>   distrustful   interested   surprised

76

PASSAGE A

1. A person who is _____, in this situation, is a person who *has no special emotional feeling*.

2. A person who is _____ is a person who *has no interest* in what is happening.

3. A person who is _____ is a person who is *happy* about something.

4. A person who is _____ is a person who *feels* a little *bothered* or *feels a little angry*.

5. A person who is _____ is a person who *hears or sees something unexpected*.

6. A person who is _____ is a person who *feels uncomfortable or confused* because of something that was said or done. In this situation the person's *face* sometimes *becomes red*.

7. A person who is _____ in something is a person who *wants to know more about it* or *wants to have more experience with it*.

8. A person who is _____ is a person who *does not completely believe what is said or done*.

9. A person who is _____ is a person whose *feelings* (or emotions) *are not calm*.

> **Threads**
>
> **Air Chief Marshal Kaset Rojananil of Thailand ordered Thai International Airways to hire more attractive stewardesses.**

TASK 2

There are many other adjectives that describe how a person feels. Work with a partner and list as many as you can.

OTHER ADJECTIVES

1. _____	6. _____	11. _____	16. _____
2. _____	7. _____	12. _____	17. _____
3. _____	8. _____	13. _____	18. _____
4. _____	9. _____	14. _____	19. _____
5. _____	10. _____	15. _____	20. _____

CHAPTER 5 THINKING ABOUT FEELINGS

IT WORKS!
Learning Strategy:
Understanding and
Using Emotions

TASK 3

Look at the chart below. Tell how you personally feel about different kinds of people. Use words from Tasks 1 and 2. Then ask two classmates how they feel about the same people. Compare your results and report your findings to the rest of the class.

EXAMPLE: Q: How do you feel about dishonest people?
A: I feel that they can't be trusted.
S/he feels that dishonest people can't be trusted.
OR
S/he does not have any special feelings, etc.

KINDS OF PEOPLE	MY FEELINGS	PERSON #1	PERSON #2
Dishonest			
Generous			
Hard-working			
Homeless			
Lazy			
Mentally ill			
Physically-challenged			
Poor			
Rich			
Stingy			
Thrifty			

TASK 4

Why do you think we feel the way we do? Where do you think our feelings came from? In groups of three or four, list the sources of our attitudes.

WHERE OUR FEELINGS COME FROM

1. _____
2. _____
3. _____
4. _____
5. _____
6. _____
7. _____
8. _____
9. _____
10. _____

PASSAGE A

As You Listen

TASK 5

Now listen to a mini-lecture about the sources of our attitudes. The lecturer listed five different sources. What are they? Were they the same as yours? What did he say is the most important one? Use abbreviations.

IT WORKS!
Learning Strategy:
Taking Notes

SOURCES OF ATTITUDES

1. _____
2. _____
3. _____
4. _____
5. _____

After You Listen

TASK 6

Based on your notes, prepare a one-minute summary/description of the sources of your attitudes. Present your remarks to the rest of the class. Answer any questions they might have.

LEARNING STRATEGY

Forming Concepts: Reading quickly to find specific information helps learners understand more efficiently and maintains our interest in what we read.

TASK 7

Read the question-and-answer magazine column about role models on page 80. According to the doctor, who are the best role models for children?

Who are our children's role models?

Q MY PRETEEN daughter worships Paula Abdul. My eight-year-old boy wants posters of Hulk Hogan on his walls. I consider these people less-than-ideal role models who exemplify nothing more than, in the first case, prettiness, and in the second, brute strength. Should I discourage my children's interest in these media figures?

A THE ENTERTAINMENT figures your children admire are not really role models but transitory heroes, somewhat larger-than-life figures whose qualities have meaning at the child's stage in life. A youngster your son's age may be feeling vulnerable and may like the idea of having someone strong and powerful, such as Hulk Hogan, looking down from his walls. Your daughter, who is on the verge of adolescence, may become enchanted with a performer who seems to personify popularity and appeal to the opposite sex. Almost certainly these heroes will be replaced by others as your children grow. Try to adopt a benign attitude; don't discourage their interest or otherwise begin a conflict over the matter.

Children's most significant role models are their parents. A child picks up, or models, his parent's patterns of behavior—how the parent deals with problems, how she responds to other people and what values guide her actions. If you are truly concerned that your son and daughter are unduly impressed by qualities you consider superficial, see if you can spend more time together as a family. Children do need and want parental involvement, and they do absorb parental lessons, even when their heroes are movie stars and pop singers.

TASK 8

Do you have any role models? Tell why that person, group, etc. is a role model for you. Use *because* in your explanation.

EXAMPLE: _____ because _____.

Compare your written sentence with others in your group.

TASK 9

Different ethnic groups sometimes have different role models. For example, some Arabic-speaking people regard the late Anwar Sadat as a person to pattern their lives after. Others disagree and think the late Gamal Abdel Nasser is a better role model. Can you give similar examples of role models from your own country? Talk and/or write about why you feel the way you do. In groups of three or four, present your views to your classmates.

Word Study

TASK 10

There are many meanings for the verb *to cover*. Here are a few:

MEANINGS

a. be enough to pay for something
b. discuss something in a lecture or course
c. form a layer all over something
d. guarantee that money will be paid by an insurance company
e. keep a gun pointed at someone who may attack
f. place something over in order to protect or hide it

g. protect someone from enemy attack
h. report on something
i. take up a land area
j. travel a distance

LEARNING STRATEGY

Forming Concepts: Using context clues will help you figure out meanings to words.

TASK 11

Read the following sentences. Match each one with one of the meanings above.

_____ 1. She *covered* the child with a blanket.

_____ 2. His head was *covered* with blood.

_____ 3. Most of the surface of the earth is *covered* by water.

_____ 4. She had to *cover* about twenty miles a day.

_____ 5. Planes from Saudi Arabia would *cover* the whole operation.

_____ 6. Don't move. I've got you *covered*.

_____ 7. Is the house *covered* in case of fire?

_____ 8. His salary does not *cover* all the expenses.

_____ 9. The last question I'd like to *cover* is number seven.

_____ 10. She was asked to *cover* the next presidential election.

IT WORKS!
Learning Strategy:
Remembering New
Material

TASK 12

Look at the word map for sources of our attitudes. In pairs or small groups try to complete it by adding sources for other things. Compare your findings.

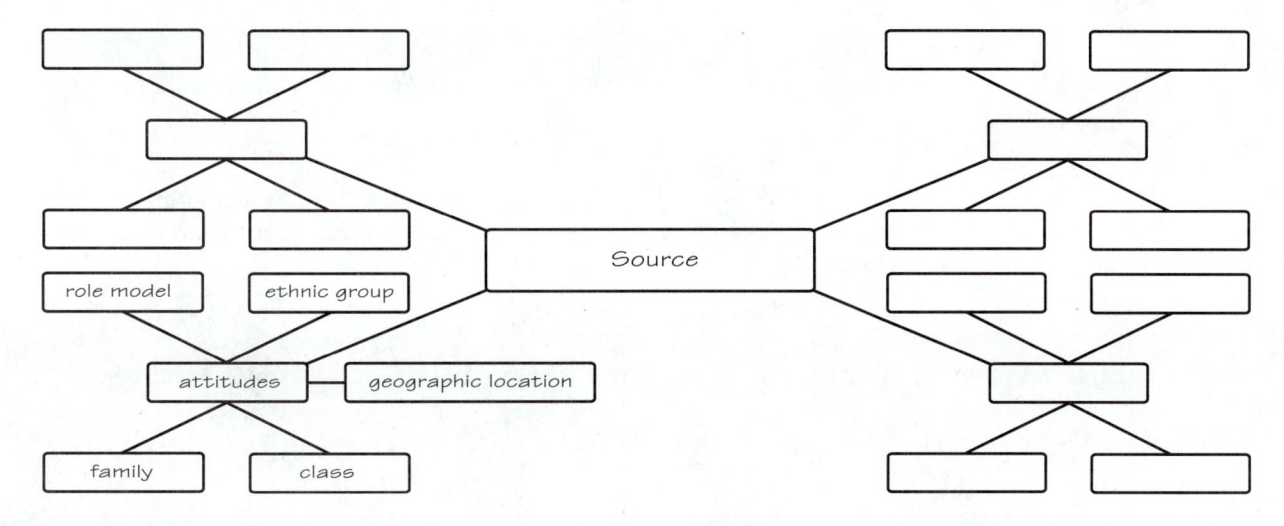

Sources of attitudes: role model, ethnic group, attitudes, geographic location, family, class → Source

PASSAGE B

IT WORKS!
Learning Strategy:
Forming Concepts

Before You Listen

TASK 13

What does *getting older* mean to you? Brainstorm for two minutes. List all the words you can think of which are associated with getting older. Compare your list with your classmates'.

_____
_____
_____
_____
_____
_____

TASK 14

The population in the United States is growing older. How do you feel about getting older? Compare your feelings with a partner.

Threads

Meals on Wheels, an organization that brings food to homebound elderly people, serves 7,700 meals every day.

TASK 15

Look at the following four topics. Talk about what each one means.

A. The Young and the Old
B. Are Older People Wiser?
C. Are Younger People Wiser?
D. Aging and Being Old

As You Listen

TASK 16

Now listen to Jim and Chuck's conversation. What was the main subject being talked about in the discussion? Choose one from the list above. Talk about your answers.

TASK 17

PASSAGE B

Listen to the discussion again and write short answers to the following questions. Talk about your answers.

1. One of the speakers compared his feelings and his thinking now to something before. What was it?
   _____
   _____

2. Who did one of the speakers say were the most intelligent people he had ever met?
   _____
   _____

3. According to one of the speakers, what happens physically to people as time passes?
   _____
   _____

4. Why is it hard for one of the speakers to think in terms of being an old person?
   _____
   _____

> **Threads**
>
> **The Weyewa tribe in Indonesia believe that you are rich if many people owe you favors.**
>
> *Milleniun: Tribal Wisdom and the Modern World* by David Maybury-Lewis (Meech Grant Productions Ltd.)

After You Listen

Word Study

TASK 18

The following sentences are from the conversation. Look at the italicized words. Practice saying them. Then, work with a partner and choose their meanings.

1. . . . if this is aging, it's really a good thing and I like it . . . so I'm *for it*.
   a. against it
   b. in favor of it
   c. afraid of it
   d. confused about it
2. . . . some of them have shown *remarkable* judgment and *remarkable* wisdom.
   a. not ordinary
   b. nice
   c. confused
   d. terrible

CHAPTER 5 THINKING ABOUT FEELINGS

3. ... I've met lots of older people, who although they weren't *senile* they were sort of spaced out ... sort of in a vacuum.
   a. hard of hearing
   b. blind and deaf
   c. strong in mind or body
   d. weak in mind or body
4. ... I've met lots of older people who, although they weren't senile they were sort of *spaced out* ... sort of in a vacuum.
   a. interested in space
   b. interested in things around them
   c. unknowing of things around them
   d. occupying space
5. ... I've met lots of older people who, although they weren't senile they were sort of spaced out ... sort of *in a vacuum*.
   a. all alone
   b. together with others
   c. in a room
   d. in a truck
6. ... they had stopped really living their lives and all they were doing was ... *recreating* old memories...
   a. asking about
   b. bringing back
   c. forgetting about
   d. watching for
7. ... they simply *were oblivious to* what was going on outside their sphere of thinking.
   a. didn't say
   b. didn't realize
   c. didn't ask
   d. didn't consider
8. ... they simply were oblivious to what was going on outside their *sphere* of thinking.
   a. specialty
   b. location
   c. globe
   d. area
9. ... I'm twenty-five which is sort of just out of *adolescence*...
   a. the adult years
   b. the happy years
   c. the sad years
   d. the teenage years

Threads

If something is presented as an accepted truth, alternative ways of thinking do not even come up for consideration.

Mindfulness, Addison-Wesley Publishers (1989)

TASK 19

Read the discussion suggestions and choose one to talk and/or write about. After you finish, present your views to the rest of the class.

- Have any of your feelings or thoughts about things changed completely in the last five years? Give examples of how you felt about something five years ago and how you feel about the same thing now. Why did you change?

PASSAGE B

- There is a saying which says that you are only as old as you feel. Do you believe this? Why? What activities can you think of which will help a person feel young?

Just for Fun

TASK 20

- Get ready for a game of "Twenty Questions" by thinking of someone you admire as a role model. Choose a person who is well-known by most people in the class—an entertainer, a politician, an educator, a world leader, etc.
- Divide the class up into two teams. A member of Team A would begin by making a statement about the person they thought of (e.g. "This person is an entertainer," or "Recently there have been many stories about this person in the news," etc.) Team B members would then try to guess the identity of the person by asking up to 20 YES/NO questions.

Name _____

Date _____

Now look at the following checklist of language learning strategies from Chapter 5. How would you assess your progress in the use of each one? Use the following symbols:

S = satisfied with progress

D = still developing

Compare yours with the instructor's assessments.

IT WORKS!
Learning Strategy:
Managing Your
Learning

LEARNING STRATEGY	MY ASSESSMENT	INSTRUCTOR'S ASSESSMENT
I am learning how to:		
remember what I hear (remembering new material)	_____	_____
understand what I hear (forming concepts)	_____	_____
express myself even though I don't know all the words (remembering new material)	_____	_____
organize and assess what I hear and say (managing your learning)	_____	_____
speak and listen to others about (understanding and using emotions)	_____	_____
learn with other people (Managing your learning)	_____	_____

ENGLISH LANGUAGE INSTITUTE
WINTERS COLLEGE 287
#29

Thinking about the Society

CHAPTER 6

WHAT'S YOUR GOAL?

IT WORKS!
Learning Strategy:
Managing Your
Learning

Look at the following four goals for Chapter 6. Which is the most important one for you? Mark it 1. How about the second most important? Mark it 2, etc.

I WANT TO LEARN HOW TO:	
A. express myself even though I don't know all the words	_____
B. organize and assess what I hear and say	_____
C. speak and listen to others about personal feelings or views	_____
D. learn with other people	_____

PASSAGE A

Before You Listen

LEARNING STRATEGY

Forming Concepts: Linking new material with past experiences promotes better understanding.

TASK 1

In a previous lesson about breast cancer, a screening process of 15 minutes was required for getting a mammogram. One questions or examines someone carefully during a screening process. Can you think of other situations in life when a screening process is used? How many can you think of? Work with a partner and list some questions for each situation.

SITUATION 1: Job Interview

POSSIBLE QUESTIONS

1. _____*Are you working now?*_____
2. _____

PASSAGE A

3. _____
4. _____
5. _____

SITUATION 2: _____

POSSIBLE QUESTIONS

1. _____
2. _____
3. _____
4. _____
5. _____

SITUATION 3: _____

POSSIBLE QUESTIONS

1. _____
2. _____
3. _____
4. _____
5. _____

> **Threads**
>
> **Thirty-four percent of the homeless population are estimated to be members of families.**
>
> U.S. Conference of Mayors, (1988)

TASK 2

Walk along the streets of any large American city and you will see homeless people. Does the place where you live have a problem with homeless people? In groups of three or four, work together and list what your community has done or what you think it has done to help solve this problem.

1. _____
2. _____
3. _____
4. _____
5. _____

*IT WORKS!
Learning Strategy:
Cooperating*

TASK 3

Look at the checklist on page 90. It will be used to screen people on the street and get them into temporary housing for a homeless village project. Talk with a partner about what each question means.

CHAPTER 6 THINKING ABOUT THE SOCIETY

	YES	NO
Are the people on the street criminals?	____	____
Are they mentally ill?	____	____
Are they working?	____	____
Are they getting help?	____	____
Do they have police records?	____	____

As You Listen

TASK 4

Now listen to a short radio news story about this screening process. Check the answers in Task 3 required to qualify for housing. Compare your results with your classmates'.

After You Listen

TASK 5

Read the newspaper article on page 91 about the homeless in Washington, D.C. and San Francisco. Talk and/or write about the reasons the articles gives for so many homeless in those cities.

IT WORKS!
Learning Strategy:
Discussing Your
Feelings

Threads

There were approximately 2.5 million fewer low-income housing units in the U.S. in 1992 than in 1980.

Institute of Medicine, (1988) p. 69

Homeless abound in San Francisco, Washington

The highest concentrations of homeless people in the United States are found in two of its most unusual cities:

- Washington, D.C., with its acres of steam grates and public property.
- San Francisco, with its history of acceptance and liberalism.

With eight homeless people for every 1,000 residents—by federal count—the two cities are far ahead of their closest rivals, Atlanta, Seattle and New York.

The specific numbers, which are based on the controversial March 1990 Census Bureau tally, are criticized as too low by people who run homeless programs, but few people dispute that San Francisco and the nation's capital top the list.

Washington's numbers may result from that city's abundant federal property and the unwillingness of federal officials to be seen rousting poor and unfortunate people. San Francisco's high concentration results from a singular combination of economic, political and geographic factors.

San Francisco, with its kind climate, long history of tolerance and reputation for fun, has been attractive to migrants of all social and economic levels since Gold Rush days.

The city's poorest people, migrants and native alike, were much less visible 15 years ago, mostly because there were many more cheap rooms for them to live in than now, experts said.

"These kinds of guys have always been with us, they just used to live in these cheap SROs (single room occupancy rooms)," said Bob Prentice, a former homeless programs coordinator for San Francisco Mayor Art Agnos.

Prentice said that redevelopment and gentrification wiped out thousands of cheap rooms during the late 1970s and early 1980s.

San Francisco Chronicle

TASK 6

Look at the following survey question and the four answers given. Ask the same question of five people you don't know. Report your findings to the rest of the class.

POINT OF VIEW

Should homeless people be allowed to sleep in public parks?

YES

Bob Miller:

Allowing the homeless to sleep in public parks would get them off the streets. If they're all together in one spot, they would be safer.

Ted Plaister:

The homeless should be allowed to sleep in parks. They just want a place to sleep. They don't want to bother anyone.

NO

Al Sasaki:

The homeless shouldn't be allowed to sleep in public parks. They might scare the children. They also might try to sell them drugs.

Rosie Holbrook:

They shouldn't be allowed to sleep in parks because we want to keep the parks clean for kids to enjoy.

CHAPTER 6 THINKING ABOUT THE SOCIETY

TASK 7

Read the following newspaper article about a plan to turn street people into farmers. Talk and/or write about the advantages and disadvantages of the plan.

A year ago, John Dixon, Tony Mastro and George Wilder were living in meat trucks, cardboard boxes and homeless shelters in New York City. Today, they are living off the land—land that could someday be theirs under a plan to turn street people into farmers.

"If someone had told me a year ago I'd be digging in the earth, I would have said they were crazy," said Dixon, 50, who lost his museum job and then his apartment in 1990 and wound up on the streets.

Now, he is a pioneer, one of the first homeless men brought to an upstate New York farm by a visionary farmer and crusader for justice, Winston Gordon.

Gordon saw the number of homeless people rising while the number of farmers fell. It was a mathematical problem for which he offered a solution: Plucking the homeless out of the city and transplanting them to his family's farm.

There they rise early and work hard, living the lives of latter-day homesteaders.

The three men are the first crop of pioneers sown by Earthwise Education Center, a non-profit group founded by Gordon, his brother Joe and organic farming advocate David Yarrow. Gordon calls it "bringing the people back home."

"On the streets, you can say, 'Well, putting money in that homeless man's cup is a dead-end street,'" he says. "Well, why not teach him to farm, then buy vegetables from him? Then he can say, 'I'm back on the streets, providing for your nutrition.'"

Earthwise is built on the premise that America has lost respect for its two greatest resources, the people and the land. It borrows ideas from new age farming, the utopian communes of the 1960s and the Iroquois Indian spirit of giving back to the land what you take out of it.

"Our Onondaga Indian friends say we must think today for seven generations," Gordon says.

The group is looking into the future of farming. Most farmers are nearing retirement, and "there's no one to take over from them," Yarrow says. Since 1981, the number of U.S. farms fell 13.7 percent, from 2.44 million to 2.1 million.

"Street people have good potential to become farmers because they're survivors," Yarrow says. "Training landless people in the methods of sustainable agriculture is laying the foundation for a new food system."

Last March, working on referrals from welfare agencies, Earthwise chose eight homeless men from New York City and brought them to Cornerstone Farm, 30 miles northeast of Syracuse. Gordon persuaded his family, who live in Chicago, to buy the 250-acre farm eight years ago.

The startup costs were minimal; the land and buildings already were there. Earthwise gets some donations and is applying for government and private grants.

The 44-year-old Gordon says he was a homeless farm laborer for 10 years himself after serving in the Air Force during the Vietnam War. He also lived in communes in the 1960s and has studied utopian experiments such as the 19th century Oneida community, just south of Cornerstone Farm.

At Cornerstone, the emphasis has been on organic farming, which produces food without chemical pesticides and puts as much nourishment back into the soil as it takes out.

Since their arrival, Dixon, Mastro and Wilder say they've become healthier and happier than ever. Wilder, who is 34 and says he was homeless for 18 years, had been an alcoholic and was in and out of hospitals.

"Eating good food, breathing fresh air. Their bodies are changing, and they don't even know it," Gordon says.

Dixon, a lifelong city dweller, says going rural was "nothing compared to the transition from self-reliance and employment to being without a job and being homeless."

At first, the homeless men had doubts. They worried they might not be able to adapt to the hard life of farming. Friends warned them they were selling themselves into plantation slavery.

"I thought, who in their right mind is going to take people off the streets and take them into live with them?" says Mastro, 34, who lost his apartment after losing his deli job last year.

Four of the eight men quickly dropped out, discouraged by the hard work. A fifth man, who had been one of the "moles" living in railroad tunnels beneath Manhattan, moved back to New York City in October and plans to marry and stay off the streets. He has a standing invitation to return to Cornerstone.

In their first season, the farm trainees planted a little of everything—beans, squash, potatoes, corn.

Next year, on the same piece of land, Dixon, Mastro and Wilder will each plant an acre on their own. Meanwhile, the Gordons and Yarrow hope to bring in 15 to 20 new homeless trainees.

Dixon, Mastro and Wilder live in a comfortable house with private bedrooms, television, stereos, books and a large common room. The Gordons and Yarrow live in the farm's main house nearby.

Gordon says he will give the men 10 acres each if they stick with the program for four years. Dixon and Mastro say they plan to take him up on it, build homes on the land and spend their lives farming. Wilder, who grew up on a farm in North Carolina, says he wants someday to buy land there and take up farming.

"This is like being a step closer to getting back to my home in North Carolina," Wilder says. "This is somewhere. It's not the middle of nowhere. Nowhere is when you're out on the street with nowhere to go."

The address for Earthwise Education Center is P.O. Box 91, Camden, N.Y. 13316.

By David Germain, Associated Press

TASK 8

PASSAGE A

Read this description of what an English teacher did to show his students what America was really like. Talk and/or write about your reactions to what the class did.

As a teacher of English to Japanese students, I am constantly exposed to the ways in which they view America; some ways are pretty strange. Most know America only through bigtime Hollywood movies. To make my students feel at home, I sometimes let them choose American names for themselves: Last summer one student wanted to be called Clint, another chose the name Arnold, and another, Sylvester.

Although this is amusing, it points out a serious phenomenon that most certainly leads to miscommunication between the two cultures. If Hollywood is the medium by which the Japanese learn about America, then the two peoples have a long way to go before there is real mutual understanding.

This summer I had the opportunity to engage in an interesting experiment while working as an English instructor in the University of Hawaii's Special English Program (SEP). I had 24 Japanese students (ranging in age from 18 to 24), most of whom had never been out of their country, take a tour of a luxury Waikiki hotel and then take a short bus ride down to the Institute for Human Services where they served lunch to Hawaii's homeless people.

It was an experiment designed to show the students several things. First, I wanted them to see the irony of America that often escapes its own citizens: people living in ultimate luxury next to others who have no home.

Next, I wanted to expose them to real life here, show them that wherever you go, people are people. I wanted them to get over their intimidation about America so that they would have a stronger desire to learn our language. Although the Hawaii Visitors bureau would definitely cringe at such a tour, each one of my students came away with an experience more rewarding than any package tour could ever provide.

Our adventure into the highs and lows of America took just two-and-a-half hours. I chose the Halekulani, which bills itself as the only five-star hotel in Waikiki, for our hotel tour. The tour guide, thinking she had some potential customers in her midst, tried to sell the hotel throughout the hour we were there. The sell-job probably wasn't necessary. The kids oohed and aahed at the hotel's pool with the orchid painted on the bottom. They expressed disbelief at the swift, smooth elevators. They smiled when fed chocolate from the hotel's own bakery. And they went crazy inside the Royal Suite, a two-bedroom luxury apartment that fetches $2,500 per night, and comes with a grand piano, a private kitchen with chef, a wrap-around ocean-front lanai and even a personal butler.

Thirty minutes after our tour of the Halekulani, my students were standing in the kitchen of the Institute for Human Services, serving over 100 free lunches to people who had no home. At first the students acted very shy. Once they started filling up the plates with food, however, they looked like old pros. Their English wasn't very good, but their diligent work and smiles made them fast friends. A couple of people picked up their lunches and said *arigato* or *konnichiwa*. the kitchen manager, Ralph, stood by with a grin. Afterward he and his staff thanked us and asked if we could come back another time.

For homework that night I had the students write about their impressions of the experience. Although their writing skills are poor at best, their honesty and sensitivity came through easily.

Kaya didn't mince words: "When I visited Halekulani and homeless people, I very surprised. There were powerful people and powerless people. I think powerful people are lonely in the heart. I feel pity for homeless. I'm happy now because I'm growing up." Tetsuya wrote: "I feel sadness and the uncertainty of life. I think humanity needs communication." Tomie wrote: "They are homeless but at first sight, looks like the common people. I wonder if they have nothing to live for."

Ayako noticed that homeless people here are treated differently than in Japan. "They are happier than Japanese homeless because Japanese don't give help to homeless and Japanese dislike homeless." Yoshiaki wrote: "I felt lonely at the IHS. There were lots of pity people. But I felt they were not gloomy. I thought they have hope. I want to do service again."

Writing of the differences between the Japanese and the American methods of helping. Maki wrote: "The Japanese form is dirty and smelly, dark and unhappy. Hawaii form is happy and clean, happy and light. I was astonished at the sight because not any homeless helpers in Japan."

Tamami was confused: "Why they have no home? It is very difficult and complicated question. America has many questions because it is so big." Miko thought she would be in danger: "I supposed homeless are fearful but they are kind." Cheiko was straightforward: "Why don't they help themselves? They aren't look homeless. There is a strange place and a strange sight. It is difficult problem to solve."

The episode proved that, contrary to what the Chamber of Commerce might think, foreigners can have memorable experiences in this country when they see beyond tourist attractions. And there are now 24 students back in Japan who no longer think Americans are all like John Wayne and Tom Cruise.

Ted Lerner

PASSAGE B

Before You Listen

TASK 9

Some think the government should give lots of direction to people. Others think people should be very free from government direction. Make a list of things you think the government *should* and *should not* control.

THE GOVERNMENT *SHOULD CONTROL* THE FOLLOWING THINGS:

1. _____
2. _____
3. _____
4. _____
5. _____
6. _____
7. _____
8. _____
9. _____
10. _____

THE GOVERNMENT *SHOULD NOT CONTROL* THE FOLLOWING THINGS:

1. _____
2. _____
3. _____
4. _____
5. _____
6. _____
7. _____
8. _____
9. _____
10. _____

Compare your lists with a classmate's. Talk about reasons for listing what you did. Report your findings to the rest of the class.

TASK 10

The United States Constitution says that Americans have the right to own guns for self-defense. Do you have the same "right" or "personal freedom" in your country? Work with a partner and discuss whether you think such a "right" is important or necessary.

Threads

On an average day, 3,836 handguns are purchased in America.

Handgun Control, Inc.

TASK 11

Read the following statements. Do you agree or disagree with each one? Why?

1. a. Most Americans do not need guns.
   b. Most Americans need guns.
2. a. Stricter laws will not prevent people from getting guns.
   b. Stricter laws will prevent people from getting guns.
3. a. More policemen are necessary to control guns.
   b. Strict laws are necessary to control guns.
4. a. Every American should be able to own a gun.
   b. Every American should be able to use a gun.
5. a. Laws to control guns would not solve any problems.
   b. Laws to control guns would solve some problems.

As You Listen

TASK 12

Now listen to four university students talk about gun control in the United States. Which of the following items were mentioned in the conversation? In groups of three or four, talk about your answers.

1. Someone says that anyone in the U.S. can buy a gun.
2. Somebody believes people will be able to get guns even if there are laws against selling them.
3. Someone once studied how to use guns.
4. Someone says owning a gun for self-defense is an American freedom.
5. Somebody mentions that many people buy guns but don't need them.

TASK 13

Look back at Task 11. Listen to the conversation again and choose which items are true for the different people in the discussion. Talk about your answers in your groups.

CHAPTER 6 THINKING ABOUT THE SOCIETY

After You Listen

Word Study

TASK 14

The following sentences are from the conversation. Look at the underlined words. Practice saying them. Then, work with a partner and choose their meanings.

1. ...there have been many attempts...to limit...guns.
   a. people have tried many times to increase the number of guns sold
   b. people have tried many times to reduce the number of guns sold
   c. people have tried many times to keep the number of guns sold the same
   d. people have tried many times to raise the price of guns
2. ...but that (trying to limit guns) runs into a lot of trouble.
   a. makes the police arrest more people
   b. makes the people fight the police
   c. causes a lot of people to buy guns
   d. causes a lot of people to oppose it
3. ...the laws that have been proposed (about guns) have not been (that) nobody can buy them...
   a. programmed
   b. predicted
   c. suggested
   d. written
4. (The proposed laws have been)...that you have to register (the guns)...
   a. go to the police station for
   b. go to the gun store for
   c. reserve a place to use
   d. make a formal written record of
5. (Not only is) the gun lobby (strong)...but (also)...the hunters...and the sportsmen...
   a. people who work to affect law makers
   b. people who work to affect gun makers
   c. people who show how to use guns
   d. people who work in gun stores
6. (People protecting themselves)...is a basic American freedom.
   a. a very important part of
   b. a very difficult part of
   c. an interesting part of
   d. an unusual part of
7. ...we have little old ladies buying guns...who are quite likely to...shoot it at the first thing.
   a. will quit using the gun
   b. will be very careful using the gun
   c. will probably fire the gun
   d. will probably like the gun

> **Threads**
>
> When a man wants to murder a tiger, he calls it sport; when a tiger wants to murder him, he calls it ferocity.
>
> *George Bernard Shaw*
> *(1856–1950)*

Following Up

TASK 15

Language which is "sexist" reflects the idea or belief that members of one sex are less intelligent or capable than those of the other. There was an example of sexist language used by one of the people in the conversation. What was it? How did the others react to it? Have you heard people in the real world make sexist remarks? What did they say? Compare answers with group members.

TASK 16

In groups of three or four, read the discussion suggestions and choose one to talk and/or write about. Afterwards, summarize discussion points and present them to the rest of the class. You could also read your paragraphs while your classmates listen and ask questions.

- Some people think owning a gun protects them from unjust government. Do you think so? What other ways can people protect themselves? Tell about any personal experiences you might have had.
- Violence in movies seems to be related to violence in real life, but no one knows the *exact* connection. What do you think? Do you believe watching violence makes people violent? Or do you think watching violence makes people lose the desire to be violent?

CHAPTER 6 THINKING ABOUT THE SOCIETY

*IT WORKS!
Learning Strategy:
Guessing*

TASK 17

Look at the fact sheet on page 98 about guns in America. Which statistic surprises you the most? What kind of group do you think published this sheet: a pro-gun organization or an anti-gun organization? How do you know? How do these facts compare with the situation in your country? Talk about your ideas with a partner.

FACTS YOU SHOULD KNOW ABOUT GUNS AND VIOLENCE IN AMERICA

- 24,020 Americans were murdered in 1991, more than any other year in our nation's history.
- In 1991, on an average day, 66 people were killed.
- 44% of all murders were committed with a handgun.
- From 1985 to 1991, the murder rate has soared by more than 25%.
- The murder toll is rising in all regions of the country and the victims represent every social and economic segment of our population.
- You are about twice as likely to be the victim of a murder today than you were in 1960.
- One out of every six guns used in crime was purchased over the counter of a gun shop or department store.
- An estimated 200 million guns are in the possession of private citizens and 60–70 million of them are handguns.
- Offenders armed with handguns committed an average of 639,000 violent crimes each year between 1979–1987.
- 72% of handgun crime victims are unknown to their assailants and 42% of such crimes occur at random on the street.
- Assault weapons are 20 times more likely to be used in a crime than any other firearms.
- Three out of every 10 guns traced to organized crime or drug cartels were assault weapons.
- The chance that you will be a victim of violent crime (with or without injury) is greater than your risk of being hurt in a car accident.

PASSAGE B

Name: _____

Date: _____

Now look at the following checklist of language learning strategies from Chapter 6. How would you assess your progress in the use of each one? Use the following symbols:

S = satisfied with progress

D = still developing

Compare yours with the instructor's assessments.

IT WORKS!
Learning Strategy:
Managing Your
Learning

LEARNING STRATEGY	MY ASSESSMENT	INSTRUCTOR'S ASSESSMENT
I am learning how to:		
express myself even though I don't know all the words (overcoming limitations)	_____	_____
organize and assess what I hear and say (managing your learning)	_____	_____
speak and listen to others about personal feelings or views (understanding and using emotions)	_____	_____
learn with other people (understanding and using emotions)	_____	_____

Saving the Planet

CHAPTER 7

WHAT'S YOUR GOAL?

Look at the following seven goals for Chapter 7. Which is the most important one for you? Mark it 1. How about the second most important? Mark it 2, etc.

IT WORKS!
Learning Strategy:
Managing Your
Learning

I WANT TO LEARN HOW TO:	
A. remember what I hear	_____
B. understand what I hear	_____
C. guess the meaning of what I hear	_____
D. express myself even though I don't know all the words	_____
E. organize and assess what I hear and say	_____
F. speak and listen to others about personal feelings or views	_____
G. learn with other people	_____

PASSAGE A

IT WORKS!
Learning Strategy:
Highlighting

Before You Listen

TASK 1

Read the following column for "good ideas" about saving the planet. Highlight interesting and important ideas.

102

Saving the planet is just a big chore

Paper or plastic? A simple question, on the surface, but one I've come to dread because no matter which one I choose, it's the wrong choice.

If I choose a paper bag, I'm killing trees. If I choose a plastic bag, I've acquired something that isn't biodegradable, that may be hanging around some landfill for the next millennium or so.

So, which should I choose?

Paper or plastic?

It's not a question for the guilt-prone. There's something about it that makes me think about all the environmentally incorrect things I do. Driving a car. Eating meat. Using an air conditioner. Putting a flea collar on my cat. Just living, more or less.

I'm not green enough. But no matter how green you are, it's never enough. There's always something else you should be doing, but aren't. Something else you could be doing, but won't. Car-pooling. Composting. Recycling gray water. Saving the rain forests. Saving the ozone layer. Saving the planet.

Paper or plastic?

Sometimes I shop at a health-food market, excuse me, a whole-food grocery store, a temple to clean living and environmental correctness. The people at this store encourage greenness in their customers. Among many other things, they sell cloth carry-bags at cost, $3.99. But in all the many times I've shopped there, I've seen very few people using cloth bags, or string bags or anything but paper or plastic bags to carry away their groceries. Why?

Why haven't I bought one of the cloth bags myself? Is it because I'm lazy? Or because I don't care? Or is it because almost every time I see somebody carting off their groceries in a cloth bag they look so virtuous, so superior, so greener-than-thou that I know I could never stand to be one of them?

I know this is stupid, but there it is. I want to be a *pro*sumer, not just a consumer, but I'm not sure I have the right attitude.

Paper or plastic?

When I hear those words I feel as though the fate of the world hangs on my decision. Lately I've been choosing plastic because the bags are so handy for other things. I suppose I could claim to be recycling them, although that's not the right reason to choose plastic over paper.

The right reason to choose plastic is that the latest exhaustive study indicates that plastic bags are less harmful to the environment than paper bags. But the study was underwritten by an association of plastics manufacturers. Should they be trusted?

"Paper or plastic?"

The man in front of me in line at the whole-food grocery store is middle-aged, nicely dressed, carrying a briefcase.

"*You* decide," he says to the person bagging his groceries.

I wonder: What's going on here? Maybe he's just come from work where he's been making decisions all day, and he can't bring himself to make another one. Or maybe he's just fed up with the question. His response seems to bewilder the young woman bagging his groceries.

"Paper or plastic?" she asks again.

"Whatever you say," he replies, amiably. But there's something about his smile as he says it. It's a little too tight, maybe even a bit hostile. Or is it my imagination?

She grabs a plastic bag and stuffs his order into it.

Plastic. An actual employee of the store chose plastic over paper. Could this be construed as an official endorsement? Or am I reading too much into it?

Diane White, MidWeek

In pairs or small groups list at least five different things from the article to help the earth. Also list how we can harm the earth. Talk about the meanings for each one.

TO HELP THE EARTH	TO HARM THE EARTH
1. _____	1. _____
2. _____	2. _____
3. _____	3. _____
4. _____	4. _____
5. _____	5. _____

CHAPTER 7
SAVING THE PLANET

TASK 2

What about your ideas? Add to the above list with some of your own. Compare and discuss with a partner.

IT WORKS!
Learning Strategy:
Sharing Ideas

MY WAYS TO HELP THE EARTH　　　**MY WAYS TO HARM THE EARTH**

1. _____　　1. _____
2. _____　　2. _____
3. _____　　3. _____
4. _____　　4. _____
5. _____　　5. _____

Now pool your ideas and report them to the rest of the class.

TASK 3

The United States is the largest user of energy of any other nation in the world. Saving energy will help the earth. Make a list of things you can do at home to save energy. Work with a partner and compare your list with other classmates.

1. _Turn off unnecessary lights_　　6. _____
2. _____　　7. _____
3. _____　　8. _____
4. _____　　9. _____
5. _____　　10. _____

> **Threads**
>
> **De-inking 100 tons of recycled paper creates 40 tons of potentially toxic sludge.**
>
> *National Wildlife Federation, 1990.*

TASK 4

How can energy be saved in all of the activities shown on pages 104 and 105? Compare answers.

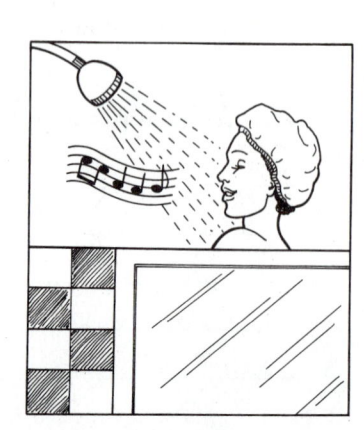

PASSAGE A

As You Listen

TASK 5

Utilities are the services we pay for to use water, gas, and electricity. What usual percentage of the monthly utility bill goes for heating water? Make a guess and then listen to the radio ad to see if you were correct.

MY GUESS _____ %

RADIO AD _____ %

IT WORKS!
Learning Strategy:
Guessing

TASK 6

Following are ways to lower the cost of heating water. What does each one mean? In groups of three or four, talk about meanings.

_____ 1. fix leaking faucets
_____ 2. install a heat pump water heater
_____ 3. insulate heating pipes
_____ 4. lower the water temperature to 120°
_____ 5. run the dishwasher only when full
_____ 6. take showers/not baths
_____ 7. use an appropriate size water tank
_____ 8. use more efficient fuels
_____ 9. use more unheated water
_____ 10. use solar energy for heating water

TASK 7

Now listen to the radio ad again and check (✓) all the ways mentioned in Task 6. Talk about answers.

After You Listen

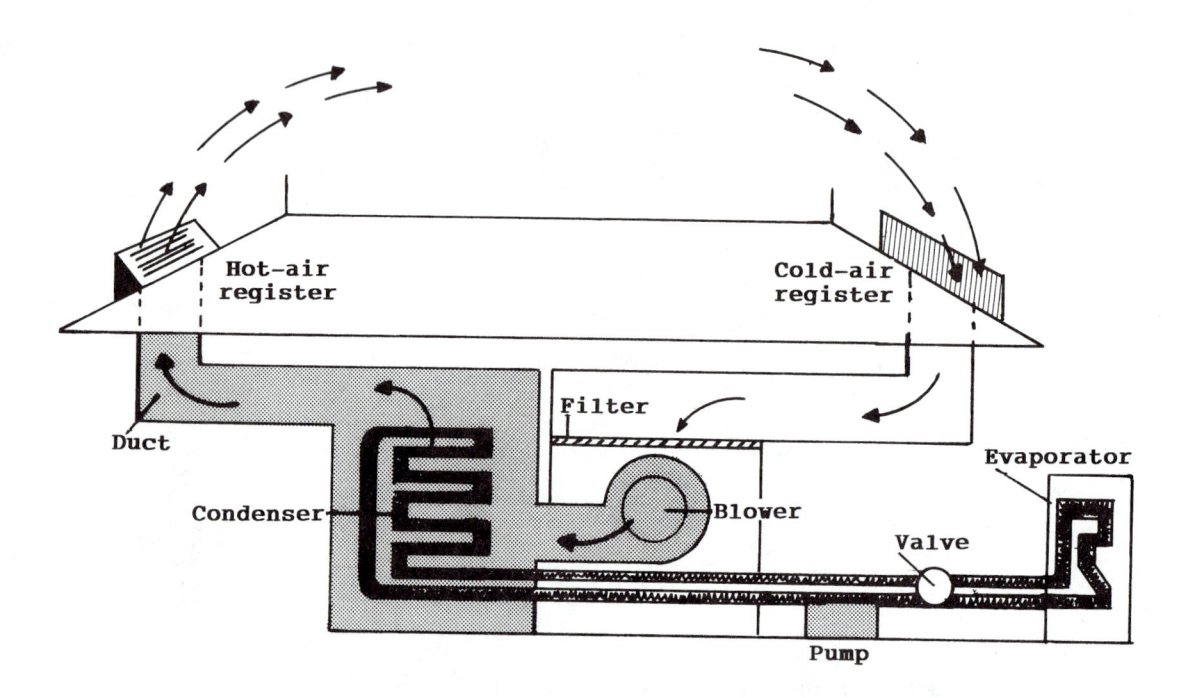

Heat pump. A heating system that uses a heat pump operates much like a warm-air system. But the heat pump uses a condenser, evaporator, pump, and other equipment to get heat from outside air or the ground and "pump" it into the building.

TASK 8

Look at this drawing of a heat pump and the diagram of a heating system used in many buildings in the northern U.S. Then read the following article about heat pumps used for heating water in Hawaii. In groups of three or four, talk and/or write about the importance of using efficient heating systems and reducing the consumption of imported oil. Afterwards, summarize discussion points and present them to the rest of the class. You could also read your paragraphs while classmates listen and ask questions.

Heat pumps for Hawaii's homes

We've had another beautiful and warm Hawaiian summer. Did you know that the warm Hawaii air can help heat the water in your home more efficiently and economically?

The residential heat pump water heater is the system that achieves efficiencies and cost savings unobtainable with conventional electric or gas fed water heaters.

The heat pump principle is quite simple—the heat pump extracts heat from the air, rises the temperature further with a compressor, and transfers the heat to the water. Since most of the energy comes from the air, the amount of heat energy transferred to the water is significantly greater than the energy consumed to operate the heat pump.

In fact, almost three times the input energy is transferred to the storage tank. The technology is simple, reliable, and proven. The result is hot water for a lot less cost.

Heat pumps have been used in Hawaii for over ten years. Since 1980 on Oahu, about 200 apartment buildings with over 30,000 apartment living units, some 19 hotels, and eight hospitals have replaced their conventional central water heating systems with heat pump water heaters.

Over 14,000 residential heat pumps have also been installed in homes on Oahu.

The residential heat pump water heater comes in two configurations. An integral unit has the heat pump mounted on the top of the storage tank.

The heat pump unit can also be purchased as a separate unit and usually is located above or on the floor next to the storage tank.

We believe a particularly good application for heat pumps is to be furnished as part of the appliances in new residential developments. Large scale installations can take advantage of volume pricing for the heat pump equipment with no significant additional installation costs.

Although the initial cost of the heat pump water heater is more than a conventional water heater, there is a state tax credit of 20 percent which offsets a portion of the cost.

Assuming a family of four, the energy savings over ten years in today's dollars is almost $2,000 when compared to a conventional gas or electric resistance water heater.

This more than offsets the higher initial cost difference of about $500 for the heat pump including the tax credit, for a net savings of $1,500. There would be similar savings over a conventional gas fired water heater.

The heat pump water heater is an energy efficient and economical system. The energy savings that the heat pump water will give to the homeowner easily pays back for the higher initial cost.

Ralph M. Imal, Director Technical Services, Hawaiian Electric Company, Inc.

TASK 9

Parks of the United States are in a drought. More and more, water is becoming too valuable to waste. Look at the chart below to see how much water is used for each of the following activities. Talk or write about some ways that people could save water at home, at school, and in their community.

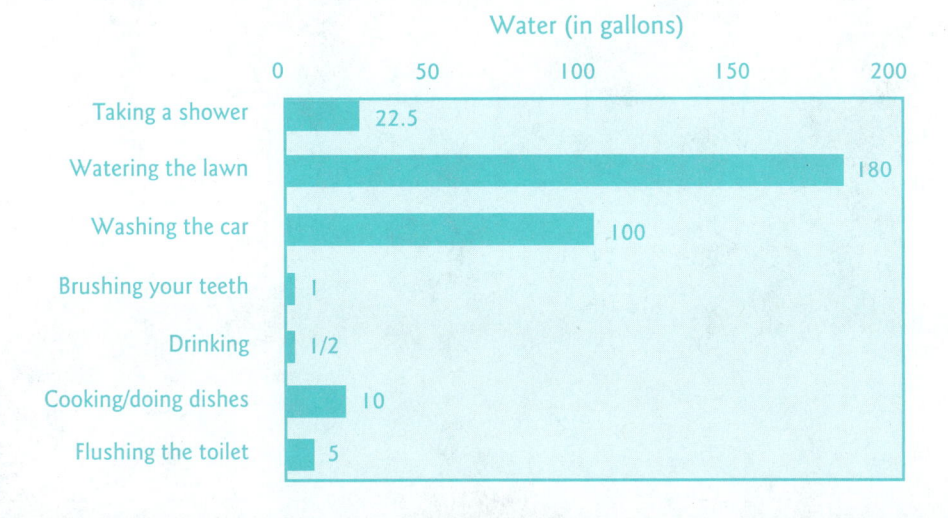

Water (in gallons)

Activity	Gallons
Taking a shower	22.5
Watering the lawn	180
Washing the car	100
Brushing your teeth	1
Drinking	1/2
Cooking/doing dishes	10
Flushing the toilet	5

PASSAGE B

IT WORKS!
Learning Strategy:
Cooperating

Before You Listen

TASK 10

Another way to save energy and money at home is to use more energy efficient appliances. Look at the following illustrations and with a partner decide which uses more energy.

REFRIGERATORS

A.

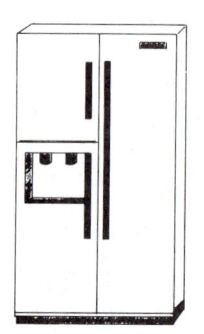

B.

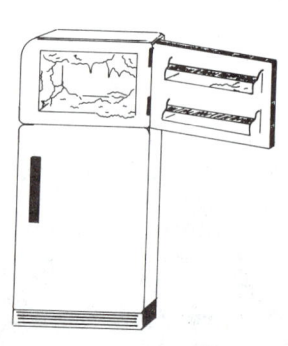

RANGES

A.

B.

LIGHTS

A.

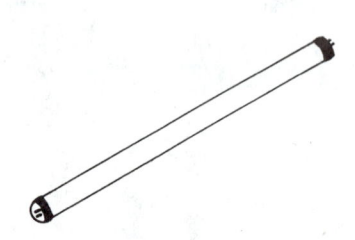

B.

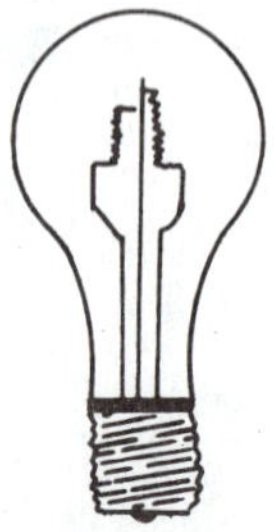

Threads

For a list of plants that fight household toxics, send a self-addressed, stamped envelope to: Foliage for Clean Air Council, 405 North Washington Street, Suite 104, Falls Church, VA 22046.

PASSAGE B

As You Listen

TASK 11

Now listen to the mini-lecture about fuel consumption and see if your guesses were correct.

TASK 12

Listen one more time and note how much more energy is used by one item over the other.

After You Listen

Word Study

TASK 13

The heat pump water heater is an *alternative* for heating water. It also saves energy. In pairs or small groups think of alternatives for the following which will also save energy. Report findings.

IT WORKS!
Learning Strategy:
Cooperating

	ALTERNATIVE	*heat pump water heater*
conventional water heater	→	_____
conventional oven	→	_____
oil/gas furnace	→	_____
electric water heater	→	_____
driving a car	→	_____
dishwasher	→	_____

Can you think of other alternatives for saving energy?

TASK 14

-Free combines with nouns to form adjectives which means "not having." For example, a *frost-free* refrigerator is one which has no ice crystals forming on the inside. How many other similar words can you think of? What does each one mean?

WORD	MEANING
1. _____	_____
2. _____	_____
3. _____	_____
4. _____	_____

CHAPTER 7 SAVING THE PLANET

TASK 15

Practice saying these words from the radio ad and the mini-lecture. In groups of three or four, talk about what they mean.

annual	conventional
alternative	defrost
appliances	depleted
consumer	harnessing
consumption	sensible

IT WORKS!
Learning Strategy:
Practicing

TASK 16

Complete the following sentences by filling in the blanks with words from Task 15. Sometimes word forms will change.

1. Be sure and look for the yellow energy saver sticker on all major _____ before you buy anything.
2. By installing a heat pump water heater, your _____ savings will amount to $380.
3. What other _____ are there for reducing our utility bill?
4. Some people consider _____ refrigerators as old-fashioned.
5. What responsibility does the manufacturer have for the _____?
6. Energy conscious individuals are worried about fuel _____ in this country.
7. Refrigerators must be _____ more frequently in warm weather.
8. One way of _____ the sun's energy is to install solar heat panels on the roof.
9. The U.S. government needs to initiate a _____ energy policy.
10. Our natural resources are being _____ at an alarming rate.

Threads

On June 25, 1991, Brazilian president Fernando Collor de Mello abolished tax subsidies for farmers and ranchers who cut down the Amazon rain forest.

Information Please Almanac,

IT WORKS!
Learning Strategy:
Remembering New Material

TASK 17

Now look at the following word relationships. Fill in the blanks with the words from the previous list. Talk about reasons for your answers.

1. *Big* is to *large* as *yearly* is to _____.
2. *Short* is to *tall* as *impractical* is to _____.
3. *Hand* is to *finger* as *society* is to _____.
4. *Bank* is to *money* as *kitchen* is to _____.
5. *Whispered* is to *shouted* as *used* is to _____.
6. *Lights* is to *turn off* as *refrigerator* is to _____.
7. *Comfortable* is to *comfort* as *alternate* is to _____.

8. *Effective* is to *efficient* as *standard* is to _____.
9. *Insulate* is to *insulation* as *consume* is to _____.
10. *Saying* is to *telling* as *using* is to _____.

Following Up

TASK 18

Have you ever seen this sticker on appliances before? Read the following magazine ad for an electric power company. Either write or call for the free booklet which tells about home costs of electricity.

PASSAGE B

IT WORKS!
Learning Strategy:
Overcoming
Limitations

This is the most important feature you should look for on a major appliance.

When you're comparison shopping, Columbus Southern power Urges you to compare the yellow Energy Guide labels affixed to major appliances. The lower the large number in the middle, the less energy the appliance will use. The numbers to the left and right show the low and high range of annual operating costs for similar size models. While the most energy efficient appliance might cost a little more initially, you'll make up the difference year after year with lower energy bills. So stick with the sticker—look at the Energy Guide label. Because the lowest sale price might not be the best bargain.

How much does it cost to use electricity in your home? Write for our free booklet "The Cost of Convenience."

Name: _____
Phone: _____
Address: _____
City: _____ State: __ Zip: _____
Mail to:
    Columbus Southern Power
    Public Affairs Dept.
    215 N. Front Street
    Columbus, OH 43215

To receive your copy of "The Cost of Convenience" even faster, call us at 1-800-327-3100

CHAPTER 7 SAVING THE PLANET

TASK 19

Read the following newspaper article about energy-saving light bulbs. Talk and/or write about how to convince people to use more energy efficient lighting in homes and businesses.

Energy-saving light bulbs being touted as pollution preventer

The wonder of the simple light bulb. It is being hailed as the way for Americans to make steep cuts in energy use, save billions of dollars, and help clean up the planet by not having to build as many polluting power plants.

But government and industry experts admit that getting people to scrap their cheap, energy thirsty lights for more efficient—and more expensive—models is not likely to be easy.

"It's a tough marketing undertaking to say the least," says Dick Dowhan, a spokesman for GTE-Sylvania, one of the country's major bulb manufacturers.

Nearly one-fourth of the electricity used in the United States goes to light offices, factories, and homes, but most of the lights are far less efficient than they could be.

If everyone were using "the technology (available) on the shelf today we could cut our electricity use at least in half," says Bob Kwartin, director of a government program called Green Lights, whose aim is to convince industry to replace inefficient lights.

He says about 400 companies, including the likes of American Express, Boeing Co., and Polaroid, have committed to upgrading their lights over the next five years.

The trick is to convince corporate executives that the initial investments will pay off in the long run. That's even harder when dealing with the average homeowner, admit energy experts, even though a growing number of electric utilities are offering to pay part of the cost for more efficient lights.

Last week the Senate approved new efficiency standards for lights in commercial buildings, factories, and some residential lights. The measure is likely to clear Congress this year.

Such standards would mean that the most wasteful lights—the conventional 40-watt fluorescent lamps still in overwhelming use today will no longer be made after a few years.

They would be replaced by a 34-watt version, that would save 15 percent of the electricity while the reduced wattage would barely be noticed. These lights have been available since the 1970s, but have been slow in penetrating the market because they are slightly more expensive, experts say.

The new standards would save enough electricity that 17 large power plants will not have to be built, saving consumers more than $25 billion over the next 20 years, says Sen. Timothy Wirth, D. Colo.

But these improvements represent only the first step in the energy saving potential in lighting experts at the American Council for an Energy Efficient Economy, a nonprofit research group.

H. Josef Hebert, Associated Press

Threads

Induction lamps have no parts to wear out and last 60 times longer than incandescent bulbs.

Just for Fun

PASSAGE B

Who cares?

Do the students at your school care about the environment? Which environmental problem concerns them most? Your class can answer the second question by taking a poll. Use the form below. If you want to include other problems, work with your classmates to create your own form.

Which Environmental Problem Concerns You Most?			
Water Pollution	**Garbage Problem**	**Destruction of Ozone Layer**	**Endangered Animals**
Total: ___	Total: ___	Total: ___	Total: ___

Using the form above, try to talk to at least 10 students. Begin by introducing yourself as a pollster. Say something like, "Hi! I'm taking a poll. Can you take a minute to answer a question?"

Ask the question at the top of the form. Then read the choices. When a student gives his or her choice, but a check mark (✓) in the correct column on your form. When you're finished polling, count the check marks in each column. Write the total number of checks for each choice.

Which environmental problem do the students at your school care about most? To find out, work with your class to combine the totals on each form. Then figure out a way to share your results with the rest of your school.

CHAPTER 7 SAVING THE PLANET

Name _____

Date _____

Now look at the following checklist of language learning strategies from Unit Seven. How would you assess your progress in the use of each one? Use the following symbols:

S = satisfied with progress

D = still developing

Compare yours with the instructor's assessments.

LEARNING STRATEGY	MY ASSESSMENT	INSTRUCTOR'S ASSESSMENT
I am learning how to:		
remember what I hear (remembering new material)	_____	_____
understand what I hear (forming concepts)	_____	_____
guess the meaning of what I hear (forming concepts)	_____	_____
express myself even though I don't know all the words (overcoming limitations)	_____	_____
organize and assess what I hear and say (managing your learning)	_____	_____
speak and listen to others about personal feelings or views (understanding and using emotions)	_____	_____
learn with other people (managing your learning)	_____	_____

Learning to Learn

CHAPTER 8

WHAT'S YOUR GOAL?

Look at the following seven goals for Chapter 8. Which is the most important one for you? Mark it 1. How about the second most important? Mark it 2, etc.

IT WORKS!
Learning Strategy:
Managing Your
Learning

I WANT TO LEARN HOW TO:	
A. remember what I hear	_____
B. understand what I hear	_____
C. guess the meaning of what I hear	_____
D. express myself even though I don't know all the words	_____
E. organize and assess what I hear and say	_____
F. speak and listen to others about personal feelings or views	_____
G. learn with other people	_____

PASSAGE A

Before You Listen

IT WORKS!
Learning Strategy:
Find a Comfortable
Place to Work

TASK 1

These students are studying in two different places. List how the places are different. Which place would you rather study in? Why? Compare your answers with your classmates' answers.

1. _____
2. _____
3. _____
4. _____
5. _____

116

PASSAGE A

TASK 2

You will hear a mini-lecture about places to study. Look at the following list of words. Practice saying them. Which words do you think you will hear? Why? Discuss your answers with a partner.

IT WORKS!
Learning Strategy:
Guessing

auditory	library
bus	music
carrel(s)	noise
clean	office
comfortable	orderly
concentrate	preferences
conditions	quiet
desk(s)	tables
distractions	variety
efficiently	visual
learn	window

Threads

There were 386,851 foreign students studying in the United States in the 1989–90 school year.

Chronicle of Higher Education, 1990.

As You Listen

TASK 3

Look at the vocabulary list above. Listen to the mini-lecture. Underline the words that you hear. Discuss your choices with a partner.

TASK 4

IT WORKS!
Learning Strategy:
Getting the Main Idea

This mini-lecture has two main ideas. Read the following sentences. Put an X in front of the two most important points. Discuss your choices. If you want, you may listen again.

_____ 1. The best place to study is where you learn best.

_____ 2. It is possible to study underneath a blanket with a flashlight.

_____ 3. Generally, a place without distractions is the best place to study.

_____ 4. The best place to study is one that is quiet.

_____ 5. The best place to study is in the library.

CHAPTER 8
LEARNING TO LEARN

After You Listen

Word Study

TASK 5

The words on the left are from the mini-lecture. Practice saying them. Match the words with their definitions on the right. Discuss your answers.

_____ 1. the particulars   **a.** ability or power to do something

_____ 2. top   **b.** best

_____ 3. I can't complain   **c.** certainly

_____ 4. like   **d.** Everything is all right.

_____ 5. energy   **e.** for example

_____ 6. in terms of   **f.** regarding

_____ 7. by all means   **g.** small points

IT WORKS!
Learning Strategy:
Practicing

TASK 6

Practice saying these words from the lecture. Some are adjectives, some are adverbs.

ADJECTIVES	ADVERBS
1. absolute	absolutely
2. basic	basically
3. particular	particularly
4. quiet	quietly
5. visual	visually
6. comfortable	comfortably
7. sensitive	sensitively

TASK 7

PASSAGE A

Read the sentences below. Write the correct forms of the words in the blanks. Words from number one on the list go with the sentences in number one below, words from number two with the sentences in number two, and so forth. Circle whether the word is an adjective or an adverb.

1. **a.** I told my instructor the _____ truth.
   adjective   adverb

   b. The library is an _____ beautiful place to study.
   adjective   adverb

2. **a.** He needs to study all the _____ subjects.
   adjective   adverb

   b. The reading room is _____ a good place to study.
   adjective   adverb

3. **a.** My friends _____ wanted to see the dormitories.
   adjective   adverb

   b. What _____ question did you want to ask?
   adjective   adverb

4. **a.** I am looking for a _____ carrel in the library.
   adjective   adverb

   b. Please speak _____ while you are here.
   adjective   adverb

5. **a.** I am bothered by too many _____ distractions.
   adjective   adverb

   b. _____ the place is an ideal room for thinking.
   adjective   adverb

6. **a.** All the books should fit _____ on that shelf.
   adjective   adverb

   b. I have a very _____ room in that hall.
   adjective   adverb

7. **a.** My hearing is quite _____ to loud noise.
   adjective   adverb

   b. My teacher _____ answered all the questions.
   adjective   adverb

> **Threads**
>
> In 1989, a male college graduate earned 42% more than a high school graduate. The female college graduate earned 53% more.
>
> Department of Commerce, Bureau of the Census

**CHAPTER 8
LEARNING TO LEARN**

*IT WORKS!
Learning Strategy:
Understanding Parts
of Words*

Read and discuss the following questions with your classmates.

TASK 8

The ending *-ory* is sometimes used to make nouns as in *observatory* or *laboratory*. The same ending is also used to make adjectives, as in *satisfactory* and *auditory*. How many other words can you think of that ends with *-ory*? Are they nouns or adjectives?

TASK 9

The lecturer said that television sets and windows could be *sight distractions* for studying. What other sight distractions can you think of?

TASK 10

The lecturer said that students should get into the *habit* of studying in the library. What other habits do you think students should get into?

TASK 11

Read the following summary of the mini-lecture. The first sentence has eight important words. The second one has three. Cross out the words that are not important. Discuss your answers.

The best place to study for students is any place where they can learn best. (8 important words) In general terms, the best place to study is one without distractions. (3 important words).

There are many different ways to take notes. Here is one way. One blank means one word. Write the important words in the blanks. USE ABBREVIATIONS AND/OR SYMBOLS IF YOU CAN. Compare your notes with your classmates' notes.

_____ _____ _____ _____:

—_____ _____ _____ _____

—_____ _____ _____

Listen to the mini-lecture one more time. Look at the notes while listening.

PASSAGE B

Before You Listen

TASK 12

Look back at the vocabulary list on page 117. Review meanings and pronunciation with your classmates.

TASK 13

Deadlines are dates or times for finishing something. What deadlines have you had to meet?

As You Listen

TASK 14

Listen to the second mini-lecture on places to study. Circle the words on page 117 that you hear. Discuss your answers with classmates.

TASK 15

This mini-lecture has two main ideas. Read the following sentences. Put an X in front of the most important points. Discuss your choices.

_____ 1. Many people like studying in a quiet, comfortable, orderly, and clean place.

_____ 2. The library is a good place to study because it has individual carrels, desks, and tables.

_____ 3. The best place to study depends upon each person's preference and varies from one person to another.

_____ 4. Occasionally, it is good to move from the usual study place to another.

_____ 5. A teacher usually corrects papers in an office.

CHAPTER 8
LEARNING TO LEARN

After You Listen

Word Study

TASK 16

The words below are from the mini-lecture. Practice saying them. Match the words with their definitions on the right. Discuss your answers.

_____ 1. combines   a. breaking in on
_____ 2. fairly   b. direction of one's thoughts
_____ 3. background   c. distance
_____ 4. interrupting   d. for the most part
_____ 5. occasionally   e. from time to time
_____ 6. attention   f. get out of
_____ 7. set   g. things of the same kind
_____ 8. break out of   h. joins together
_____ 9. within   i. in not more than

> **Threads**
>
> In 1992, the average cost of tuition at a public college in the United States was $5,929 and $13,422 at a private college.
>
> *Peterson's Guides Annual Surveys of Undergraduate Institutions*

TASK 17

Some of these words are from the mini-lecture. Working with a partner, look at each group and circle the word or phrase which does not belong. What reasons do you have for your answers?

1.	brings together	combines	mixes	separates
2.	fairly	rather	seldom	somewhat
3.	circumstances	conditions	projects	situations
4.	breaking in on	interrupting	stopping	studying
5.	break out of	escape	get out of	suspect
6.	desires	distractions	likes	preferences
7.	carrels	chairs	desks	tables
8.	changes	is different	prefers	varies

Read and discuss the following questions with your classmates.

PASSAGE B

TASK 18

You can add *-ion* to many English verbs to make them nouns. Some examples are:

>   distract   →   distraction
>   concentrate   →   concentration
>   interrupt   →   interruption

Can you think of some others?

TASK 19

The lecturer said there was a *great variety of preferences* about where people liked to study. Can you think of other things where there is a variety of preferences?

TASK 20

Read the following summary of the mini-lecture. Decide which words are the most important. The first sentence has nine important words. The second one has three. Cross out the words that are not important. Discuss your answers.

One cannot say there is a best place to study for most people because it varies from one person to another. (9 important words) Occasionally, it is important to vary one's study place. (3 important words)

There are many different ways to take notes. Here is one way. One blank means one word. Write the important words in the blanks. USE ABBREVIATIONS AND/OR SYMBOLS IF YOU CAN. Compare your notes with your classmates' notes.

_____ _____ _____ _____:

—_____ _____ _____ _____ _____

—_____ _____ _____

Listen to the mini-lecture one more time. Look at the notes while listening.

PASSAGE C

Before You Listen

TASK 21

There are many different ways to study a textbook. Make a list of all the things you usually do. Compare your list with your classmates' list.

1. _____
2. _____
3. _____
4. _____
5. _____
6. _____

> **Threads**
>
> "They know enough who know how to learn."
>
> Henry Adams

TASK 22

You will hear a mini-lecture about how to study a textbook. Look at the following list of words. Practice saying them. Which words do you think that you will hear? Why? Discuss your answers with a partner.

asking questions	made up	recite
a system of studying	margin	reflecting the material
code name	memory tool	review
every other paragraph	mental steps	short-term memory
first paragraph	overview	skim
first sentence	prior thinking	step
headings	question	study system
learning system	read	survey
long-term memory	recitation of ideas	technique

As You Listen

TASK 23

Look at the vocabulary list in Task 22. Listen to the mini-lecture. Underline the words that you hear. Discuss your choices with a partner.

125

PASSAGE C

TASK 24

This mini-lecture has four main ideas. Read the following sentences. Put an X in front of the four most important points. If you want, you may listen again.

_____ 1. Many study systems have been developed over the years.

_____ 2. The Cornell System is the most thorough way of studying a textbook.

_____ 3. The Cornell System has eight different steps.

_____ 4. It is important to recite aloud the main ideas that have been read.

_____ 5. The 3R System is the oldest way of studying textbooks.

_____ 6. The SQ3R Study System is the most frequently used way of studying a textbook.

_____ 7. The SQ3R Study System has five steps.

_____ 8. To improve test scores, it is important that everyone develops a system for studying.

TASK 25

Look at the phrases below. They tell you that main ideas or important points will follow. Listen to the mini-lecture again. It has been divided up into four parts. Circle the phrase which introduces the main idea that you hear for each part. Discuss your answers.

1. The critical factor is . . .
2. The most efficient study system of all is
3. . . . the most important technique . . . is
4. The most thorough . . . is
5. . . . the next method . . . is called
6. . . . the oldest one . . .
7. . . . there are some techniques that really help a lot . . .

TASK 26

The lecturer mentioned three different systems for studying a textbook. Listen again and fill in the different steps for each system. Use abbreviations. Compare your notes with a partner's notes.

THE CORNELL SYSTEM

1. _____   5. _____
2. _____   6. _____
3. _____   7. _____
4. _____   8. _____

THE 3R SYSTEM

1. _____
2. _____
3. _____

THE SQ3R SYSTEM

1. _____
2. _____
3. _____
4. _____
5. _____

After You Listen

Read and discuss the following questions with your classmates.

TASK 27

The lecturer talked about the Cornell and SQ3R Study Systems, ways to study a textbook. What other *systems* in general can you think of?

TASK 28

The SQ3R Study System is a technique for studying. What *techniques* can you think of for the following:

- memorizing telephone numbers?
- giving up smoking?
- removing lint from a black shirt?

Following Up

IT WORKS!
Learning Strategy:
Highlighting

TASK 29

Read the following article entitled "Race, Class, and College Success." With a partner, indicate the main points by highlighting only the most important words. Choose one of these important points to talk or write about. Afterwards, summarize discussion points and present them to the rest of the class. You could also read your paragraphs while your classmates listen and ask questions.

PASSAGE C

Race, Class, and College Success

According to a new report by the American Council on Education (ACE), students who enroll at a four-year college immediately after high school and stay in school continuously are far more likely to earn baccalaureate degrees than those who delay starting, take a break from their studies, or enroll in other kinds of postsecondary institutions.

The analysis shows that the likelihood that a student will take the traditional path is directly related to socioeconomic status, and that Black, Hispanic, and American Indian students are least likely to enroll full-time immediately after high school and earn a degree within six years.

These findings "raise important issues of social equity and economic policy for federal and state officials," says ACE President Robert H. Atwell, particularly in light of rising tuitions and cuts in the value of student aid.

Of all racial and ethnic groups, Asian Americans (76 percent) are the most likely to pursue some type of postsecondary education immediately after high school, followed by whites (50 percent), Blacks (42 percent), Hispanics (39 percent), and American Indians (35 percent).

Copies of *College Going, Persistence, and Completion Patterns in Higher Education: What Do We Know?* are available from: ACE, Division of Policy Analysis and Research, One Dupont Circle, Washington, DC 20036-1193 (202)939-9450.

TASK 30

In groups of three or four, look at this article which appeared in a faculty newsletter. Do you believe educational standards in Asian countries are far ahead of Western countries? Why? Give personal examples to prove your point.

IT WORKS!
Learning Strategy:
Sharing Opinions

Asians "Best" In U.K., Too

It's not just happening in the U.S. Overseas students for the first time have now outstripped British undergraduates in competition for the best degree results at universities. Students (mainly from Asia) for the first time have earned a higher percentage of top awards in higher education than "home students." **Sig Prais,** senior research fellow at the National Institute of Economic and Social Research, offered these familiar words: "Standards in countries such as Japan and Hong Kong are way ahead of those in our classrooms. The targets set for 16-year-olds in math and science are pathetic when compared with those abroad."

**CHAPTER 8
LEARNING TO LEARN**

Name _____

Date _____

*IT WORKS!
Learning Strategy:
Managing Your
Learning*

Now look at the following checklist of language learning strategies from Chapter 8. How would you assess your progress in the use of each one? Use the following symbols:

S = <u>s</u>atisfied with progress

D = still <u>d</u>eveloping

Compare yours with the instructor's assessments.

LEARNING STRATEGY	MY ASSESSMENT	INSTRUCTOR'S ASSESSMENT
I am learning how to:		
remember what I hear (remembering new material)	_____	_____
understand what I hear (forming concepts)	_____	_____
guess the meaning of what I hear (forming concepts)	_____	_____
express myself even though I don't know all the words (remembering new material)	_____	_____
organize and assess what I hear and say (managing your learning)	_____	_____
speak and listen to others about personal feelings or views (understanding and using emotions)	_____	_____
learn with other people understanding and using emotions)	_____	_____

Appendix: Each One/Teach One

EACH ONE/TEACH ONE

TASK 1

During the term everyone in the class will be working in groups on extra lessons to present to the rest of the class toward the end of the semester. Look at the following listening passages. Which one would you like to prepare lesson materials for? The class should be divided into six different topic discussion groups.

1. Conversation (2:05)
   Topic: being married
2. News Story (1:05)
   Topic: unemployment
3. Ad (50 seconds)
   Topic: appeal for blood from the Red Cross
4. News Story (45 seconds)
   Topic: household wastes
5. News Story (40 seconds)
   Topic: inaugural flight of an airline
6. Paired Mini-Lectures (2:55 2:20)
   Topic: good students

TASK 2

Look at the tapescript of the listening passage you chose. (Or, for more listening practice, transcribe the listening passage yourselves.) Talk about possible activities you might want your classmates to do. Listen and follow along with the tapescript to get more ideas.

TASK 3

Decide which members of your group will work on activities for the following areas:

BEFORE YOU LISTEN

AS YOU LISTEN

AFTER YOU LISTEN

TASK 4

Look at the following sample pages. They are organized in the same way as the rest of the textbook. If you want, you may follow this general outline in writing your own lessons.

Before You Listen

TASK 1

TASK 2

TASK 3

TASK 4

APPENDIX A
EACH ONE/TEACH ONE

As You Listen

TASK 1

TASK 2

TASK 3

TASK 4

After You Listen

Word Study

TASK 1

TASK 2

TASK 3

TASK 4

APPENDIX A
EACH ONE/TEACH ONE

Following Up

TASK 1

_____
_____
_____
_____
_____
_____

TASK 2

_____
_____
_____
_____
_____
_____

TASK 3

_____
_____
_____
_____
_____
_____

TASK 4

_____
_____
_____
_____
_____
_____

Just for Fun

TASK 1

___

TASK 2

___

TASK 3

___

TASK 4

___

APPENDIX A
EACH ONE/TEACH ONE

TASK 5

For each activity you prepare, think about the learning strategy you want your classmates to use. Choose strategies from the following list:

Understanding and Using Emotions
Managing Your Learning
Forming Concepts
Remembering New Material
Overcoming Limitations